Church History Through the Saints

SAINTS

SAINTS ARE PEOPLE

Rev. Alfred McBride, O. Praem.

Religious Education Division
Wm. C. Brown Co. Publishers
Dubuque, Iowa

Nihil Obstat:
  Rev. William G. McLaughlin

Imprimatur:
  † James J. Byrne, S.T.D.
  Archbishop of Dubuque

May 5, 1981

Cover and Design
Craig M. Brown

Production Editor
Margaret A. Shepard

CONTENTS

Jewish Christianity

Established Christianity

Reconstruction Christianity

Medieval Christianity

Renaissance Christianity

Church In Transition

USA Christianity

"The followers of Christ are called by God, not according to their accomplishments, but according to his own purpose and grace. They are justified in the Lord Jesus, and through baptism sought in faith, they truly become sons of God and sharers in the divine nature. In this way they are really made holy.

They are urged by the Apostle to live "as becomes saints" (Eph. 5,3), and to put on as God's chosen ones, holy and beloved, a heart of mercy, kindness, humility, meekness, patience (Col 3,12), and to possess the fruits of the Spirit unto holiness.

All the faithful of Christ, of what ever rank or status, are called to the fullness of Christian life and to the perfection of love. By this holiness, a more human way of life is promoted in our earthly society.

In order that the faithful may reach this perfection, they must use their strength, according as they have received it, as a gift from Christ. In this way, they can follow in his footsteps and mold themselves in his image, seeking the will of the Father in all things, devoting themselves with all their being to the glory of God and the service of their neighbor.

In this way too, the holiness of the People of God will grow into an abundant harvest of good, as is brilliantly proved by the lives of so many saints in Church History."

Vatican II, THE CHURCH, #40

"It is one thing to live with the saints in glory.
To live with them on earth is another story."

1

Peter

A Most Human Leader

"Never pay back one wrong with another, or an angry word with another one. Instead, pay back with a blessing."

I Peter 3, 9

The grandeur of Michelangelo's basilica in Rome, towering over Peter's tomb is a long way from the simple cottage where Peter was born in the fishing village of Bethsaida near Galilee lake. Son of Jona (Bar-Jona) and brother of Andrew, Peter followed in the fisherman tradition of his family.

Andrew introduced Peter to Jesus, who called him to be an apostle. Of all the apostles, the most is known about Peter. He is mentioned 195 times in the New Testament, as contrasted with 130 references to the other 11 apostles.

Originally known as Simon, his name was changed to Peter (Cephas) by Jesus. "Andrew took Simon to Jesus. Jesus looked hard at him and said 'You are Simon, son of Jona; you are to be called Cephas'— meaning rock" (Jn 1, 42).

From the beginning, Peter acts like a leader. He tends to be the spokesman for the apostles, asking Jesus the meaning of puzzling parables and correctly identifying the meaning of Jesus when asked. Jesus preaches from Peter's boat and stays at Peter's house. Jesus discusses with Peter the problem of paying Temple tax and then sends Peter to catch the fish in whose mouth is the coin used to pay the tribute.

Jesus places the leadership of the Church in Peter's hands and reconfirms this at the Last Supper: "I have prayed for you Simon (Peter) that your faith may not

3

fail, and once you have recovered, you in your turn must strengthen your brothers" (Lk 22, 32).

There is a "firstness" about Peter that cannot be evaded. Peter is the first apostle to see the Risen Lord, the first man to preach the Gospel after Pentecost, the first disciple to perform a miracle. Peter takes the lead in defending Christ and Christians before the Sanhedrin and baptizes the first gentile convert, Cornelius. And, at the Council of Jerusalem, it is Peter who convinces the assembly that gentiles have the right to become Christians without being forced to embrace circumcision and Mosaic laws about "kosher" food.

New Testament scholars see in Peter a "trajectory" of images, all pointing to his leadership role in the Christian community: The Great Christian *Fisherman;* the *Shepherd* who will feed the lambs; and *the Receiver of Special Revelations* on the mount of the Transfiguration, in hearing the case of Ananias and Sapphira, and in the vision of the unclean food. Peter has the image of the *Confessor of True Faith* at Caesarea Phillipi; and *Guardian* against false teaching, by his own testimony in 2 Peter 1, 20–21.

All this leadership talk focuses on the fact of a *Petrine Ministry* in the New Testament Church. The life of Peter supports the conclusion that it was Christ's will that there be one person who serves as a minister to the total Christian community. Such a minister-leader works together with and listens to and consults with others as did Peter.

Peter's credibility as a leader becomes all the more appealing when seen against the backdrop of his noticeably human personality—impulsive, inadequate, faltering, yet able to repent. He wanted to walk on water, but he sank in the waves and screamed in fear, he a man of the sea. This is no invincible leader.

He views the glory of the Transfiguration and distractedly thinks of housing for the three figures. Not

4

content to rest in contemplation before the wondrous beauty, he plans to capture it in a tent shrine. Manly, brave and protective, he assures Jesus that no one will ever cause Jesus suffering and death so long as the courageous Peter is guarding him. Not until Jesus calls Peter a "tempting Satan" is he convinced otherwise. These vignettes disclose a Peter lacking in some of the insight that a leader should have, and at the same time willing to be corrected and grow.

Remorselessly practical, he wants a body count on how often he should be charitable. He seems slow to grasp Christ's advice never to restrict the number of charitable deeds. Peter vows to stand by Jesus and "drink the cup of pain." Instead he falls asleep at the crucial hour and becomes so nervous at Christ's arrest that he cravenly denies he even knows who Jesus is. While Jesus takes an oath before the High Priest about his divine Sonship, Peter swears an oath to some taunting servant women that he has no idea who Jesus is.

The remarkable aspect of this story and some of the others cited is that the Gospels tell so many details that show when Peter did not act like a leader, or was deficient in the qualities one would like to ascribe to an ideal leader. One might conclude that the New Testament was not trying to whitewash Peter and thus present an ideal leader. It seems reasonable to conclude that the authors were attempting to portray a real leader who might at once be brave and fearful, sometimes insightful and occasionally blind, capable of passionate loyalty and yet prone to slip, able to sin and yet willing to repent.

In the "denial scene" we encounter a leader not yet strong enough to lead. But in the repentance that follows we get in touch with a man big enough to admit he was wrong and ready to shed tears of repentance. We may feel a greater sense of Peter's leadership potential here than in the triumphant scene at Caesarea Phillipi when he spoke with such firm assurance about the identity of Jesus.

It is quite common for authors to linger at Caesarea Phillipi and expand on how this moment emphasized Peter's leadership role. And, after all, the words of that scene are inscribed at the base of the dome of St. Peter's basilica in Rome: "You are Peter, and on this rock I will build my Church. And the gates of hell shall not prevail against it" (Mt 16: 18). The emphasis is correct, but perhaps not quite as moving as the commissioning to leadership found in John 21. The scene in Matthew has all the commanding overtones of an authoritative event. The event in John locates the call with the warmth of a Christian relationship.

The time seems to be Monday morning after Easter. Eight of the disciples had spent the whole night fishing and caught nothing. In the dawn's early light Jesus stands on the beach, unrecognized by the disciples. Jesus asks them if they have caught anything. They answer, "No." Jesus says, "Throw your nets to the starboard side and you will find something." Following his direction, they net a huge catch. Peter is the first to recognize Jesus: "It is the Lord." Peter, who had practically nothing on, wrapped his cloak around himself, jumped into the water and swam to Jesus. Neither the awkwardness of the moment, nor any self-recriminating embarrassment—nothing—no obstacle would hold Peter back from reaching the one whom his heart loved.

After a meal on the shore, Jesus spoke to Peter.

"Peter, do you love me?"

"Yes."

"Peter, do you love me more than all these others?"

"You know I love you."

"Peter, do you love me?"

Then Peter grew upset at being asked a third time. There was no doubt in his heart that he loved Jesus. "Lord, you know everything. You know that I love you."

Peter had denied Christ three times. Now he corrected those three failures to love by a triple affirmation of affection. It is in this context of healing and love that John describes the call of Peter to leadership. For every declaration of love by Peter, Jesus deepens his invitation to leadership:

"Feed my lambs . . . Look after my sheep . . . Feed my sheep."

Seldom has history recorded a more touching call to a leadership position. Here is a vision of leadership that is grounded in love and affection between the leader and Christ, and between the leader and his potential followers. This "love model" of leadership deserves more attention in discussions about the "Petrine Ministry" both because it has a sound New Testament basis and reflects the central ethical and spiritual message of the Gospel.

This Easter scene at the beach discloses a vision of leadership that flows from an adult view of loving union, trust and respect. Jesus takes the risk publicly to ask Peter for an avowal of love. He makes no comment on the denials. He does not look for groveling or apologies. He simply voices a candid appeal for affection. Peter catches the precise dignity of the moment, the fresh opportunity of being born again. His failures and weaknesses he puts behind him. He has done his weeping and confessed his sins. This Easter dawn is the beginning of a new creation, a new Peter who sings out unabashedly his love for Christ.

No wonder Jesus would choose a man of this calibre for a leader. At Caesarea Phillipi Peter showed mental sharpness in sizing up the meaning of Jesus. At the Galilee beach Peter displays an even more attractive quality, the ability to announce his love for Jesus with no holds barred and with the humbling memory that had failed in this before, but now with a powerful new feeling that he would not fail again.

He didn't. He accepted leadership—the Petrine Ministry, as some theologians like to call it—and remained lovingly faithful to Jesus until his own martyrdom in the Circus of Nero in Rome, some thirty years later. This is a leadership and ministry that Catholics believe lives on in the successors of Peter as bishops of Rome and Popes of the Catholic Church. A leadership of love and service and ministry to "all people of good will," as so beautifully expressed by John XXIII.

Reflection

Franco Zefferelli's "Jesus of Nazareth" provides an attractive insight into Peter as *leader in faith* in the scene of Magdalene's news about the Resurrection. She finds the apostles resisting the truth of her message. Frustrated and angry she leaves them with these words, "He is risen. He told me to tell you. I have done so."

Then Thomas, portrayed as chief doubter, tests the apostles. "John, do you believe her? Matthew? Andrew? . . . Peter?" Peter stands as the first apostle to believe in the Resurrection, "Yes, I do." Thomas baits him, "You? Peter. Why you denied him."

The rumble and roar of sea-swells infuse Peter's faith testimony. "Yes, I denied him. But so did we all. We ate with him. We lived with him. We knew him. Yet we abandoned him. Yes, I believe he is risen. I have always believed in him. And I know in my heart he has forgiven me. Forgiven all of us. You ask me if I believe. Yes . . . I do."

This leadership in faith, like leadership in love form the twin poles of the Petrine Ministry. It is an example for all ministers of the Christian community, wherever they may be.

Paul

He Had It All

"You have a permanent place in my heart, and God knows how much I miss you all, loving you as Christ Jesus loves you."

Phil 1, 7

God could hardly have picked a better city in which to raise and train Paul, also known as Saul, than Tarsus, a trade center in which the cultures of East and West met in a colorful and productive clash. Situated in what is modern-day Turkey, Tarsus served as a link between Persia (Iran) and the western trading peoples.

Alexander the Great conquered the city in 334 B.C. and brought to it Greek culture and education. He also planted a Jewish colony there to stimulate industry and commerce.

Pompey conquered the city for the Romans in 64 B.C. He gave the people Roman citizenship, endowed them with self-government, and encouraged civic mindedness.

From the goats grazing on the Taurus mountains overlooking the city came the raw material that was woven into haircloth, still known for its strength and durability, that was used by the tentmakers on the "Street of the Weavers"—a street that still exists in Tarsus (now called Tarsoos).

Young Saul grew up in this cosmopolitan city, where he attended a Greek university, enjoyed Roman citizenship, absorbed democratic ideals, learned to be a tentmaker and mastered both the Greek and Hebrew languages. This was also the city where he assimilated many of his ideas about women and their place in society, for here he encountered women with faces veiled who were treated according to customs imported from Persia.

The final stage of his education was completed in Jerusalem where he studied to become a Pharisee. He was a student of Gamaliel, a tutor whose views were sensible, compassionate, and moderate. It is altogether possible that Paul would have been in Jerusalem at the same time Jesus visited the city, but no record exists of their meeting one another.

God prepared Paul very well for the worldwide mission that lay before him. Bilingual, bicultural, equipped with Greek and Jewish education, Paul was ideally suited to bring to Christianity its universal calling.

The final readying occurred on the Road to Damascus. Though Paul was a student of the temperate Gamaliel, he was far more passionate and strict than his mentor. He stood by in approval when fellow Jews stoned the Christian deacon Stephen to death. Now he had become aggressive in stamping out those with faith in Jesus.

Together with some Temple policemen, Paul traveled one hundred forty miles from Jerusalem to Damascus. He carried extradition papers from the High Priest, allowing him to arrest Damascus Christians and bring them back to Jerusalem for trial and possible execution. At the end of the seven-day journey, Paul and his companions reached the height of the road of Mt. Hermon, overlooking the white city of Damascus, set in a green plain, described by some as a "handful of pearls in an emerald goblet."

Suddenly a blinding light struck Paul, knocking him to the ground. He heard a voice saying, "Saul, Saul, why are you persecuting me?" He asked, "Who are you, Lord?" The voice answered, "I am Jesus, and you are persecuting me. Get up now and go into the city, and you will be told what you have to do."

His comrades brought him to Straight Street, where the Lord sent Ananias to baptize Paul and give him a brotherly welcome into the Christian community.

According to Galatians 1: 17, Paul then went into seclusion for three years in the Arabian desert. As Jesus went into the desert to pray, so also Paul went to the desert to be alone with God, to probe the meaning of his Damascus experience and absorb its impact. Here he was to have another stunning experience of God, which he described in these words, "I will move onto visions and revelations I have had from the Lord. I know a man in Christ who was caught up into the third heaven . . . caught up into paradise and heard things which must not and cannot be put into human language" (cf. 2 Cor. 12:1-6).

While Paul was enjoying such ecstasies in the Arabian wilderness, he was rudely jolted by the appearance of a mysterious "thorn in the flesh." As he says, "In view of the extraordinary nature of these revelations, to stop me from getting too proud I was given a thorn in the flesh, an angel of Satan to beat me and stop me from getting too proud" (2 Cor. 12:7).

What was this thorn? Body sores? Eye infections? Sexual torment? Incessant persecution and nonacceptance? We will never know. What is clear is that it was severe enough to bother him and humble him fourteen years later when he wrote the above words.

After the years in Arabia, Paul began his missionary work, preaching the love of Christ in the synagogue of Damascus. Here he knew his first success and his first rejection. So angry did some people get with him that he had to escape in a basket from the city.

He decided to go to Jerusalem and meet Peter and the other apostles of Jesus. It was important to him to gain acceptance and affirmation from them. But given his former reputation, he inspired fearful hesitation and doubt in the Christian community. It took Barnabas,

whose name means "son of encouragement," to calm
the community enough to be open to the truth of Paul's
conversion.

So the giants of Christianity met one another. Paul,
the wiry rabbinical student, and Peter, the rough-hewn
fisherman. They took measure of one another, accepted
each other as brothers, and spent fifteen days together
in Jerusalem. Peter shared with Paul the warm and
vivid details of the life of Jesus.

Peter brought Paul to places made memorable by the
deeds of Jesus—the pool of Siloam; the place where
the woman was taken in adultery; and the rich man's
house where Magdalene washed Christ's feet. They
walked through the Temple, and Paul heard how Jesus
cleansed it. They stood before the house of Caiphas,
the Praetorium of Pilate, and the pillar of the
scourging. They walked the Via Dolorosa—the Way of
the Cross—and knelt at Calvary. They prayed at the
tomb of the Resurrection.

In turn, Paul shared with Peter and the others his
religious experiences on the Damascus Road and in the
Arabian wilderness. This faith-sharing between Peter
and Paul bound them so closely as spiritual brothers
that the Church celebrates their feasts together on the
same day, June 29.

At the end of this two-week visit, one might think
that Paul was ready to conquer the world. Anointed
from heaven and confirmed by Peter, what other
preparation would he need? Peter judges that Paul
needs more tempering. Allied to this is Peter's belief
that the young Christian community needs to move
more slowly in this stabilizing period. Paul's boiling
ardor would move things too fast. Paul's "hour" had
not yet come.

Hence Peter advises Paul to return to Tarsus and
await a call from the Church. This must have been an
incredibly frustrating experience for Paul. A missionary
with no mission. Gifted with matchless revelations,
honored by the approval of Peter, he would go home to

a city where his old friends would cold-shoulder him and the synagogue shut its doors to him. The world's most eloquent preacher would spend his days making tents. The man who became the world's greatest missionary was asked by the Church to accept a "ministry of silence" for four years. He saw the Church moving on without him. In faith and obedience he contained his monumental impulses and energies and offered his prayer and silence for the success of others.

Four years later, the Church was ready to open a mission to the Gentiles of Antioch. Peter sent Barnabas to Tarsus to call Paul out of seclusion. Paul's "hour" of liberation had come. From then on nothing could contain the whirlwind that was Paul's passion for missionary work. As the sea breezes filled the sails of his boat to Antioch, Paul stood stalwart and exulted, "I am certain of this: neither death nor life, no angel, no prince, nothing that exists, nothing still to come, not any power or height or depth, nor any created thing can come between us and the love of God made visible in Christ Jesus our Lord" (Rom 8, 38–39).

Reflection

Paul is so well known as an evangelizer, missionary, and minister of the Word that it is easy to forget he spent seven years in prayer and contemplation before embarking on a career that would make him the "second founder" of Christianity. Paul the mystic stands behind Paul the activist. First he was "into" Christ Jesus before he preached about him. The deeper the preparation, the more profound the results. With the exception of Jesus, there probably has never been so penetrating a combination of mystical prayer and active ministry as in Paul. We tend to see his work and forget his prayer. We will do well to remember both.

At the same time Paul is no stranger to the need for assuring the permanence of the Church. He undertook three missionary journeys in which he established mission stations—or churches—in Lystra, Iconium, Derbe, Troas, Cyprus, Phillipi, Ephesus, Corinth, and so forth. But he did more than just make converts. He also created structures that would keep the churches going after he left them. One of the principal reasons for his epistles was to keep in touch with his converts and strengthen them for the future.

Unlike some idealists who have no practical know-how, and different from those "nuts and bolts" people who are utterly impatient with dreamers and wooly idealists, Paul was at once the supreme idealist and the consummate practical man. His passion extended beyond sermons so eloquent that they made countless converts. He could be just as passionate in taking up collections for the churches, solving quarrels and dilemmas in local congregations, appointing pastors for the mission stations and attending to other administrative details needed for rooting permanent Christian communities.

In many ways, "Paul had it all." One can barely calculate his influence on Christian theology. All subsequent Christian theologians, including Augustine, Aquinas, Luther, and Calvin have been influenced profoundly by Paul. Author Michael Hart ranks Paul as the sixth most influential man in history. (He ranks Jesus third). Christians are likely to think otherwise, placing Christ at the very center of history and Mary his Mother next to him.

One may argue that Paul is a close third.

John Chrysostom

(347–407)

An Eloquent Moralizer

"Preaching makes me healthy. As soon as I open my mouth, all tiredness is gone."

Chrysostom, Homily Comment

In the spring of 387, a tax riot erupted in Antioch. The emperor had ordered the citizens to make a heavy contribution to the defense budget, providing five gold pieces for each soldier of the imperial army. The people mounted a tax revolt. Mobs vandalized the Baths of Caligula, stormed the governor's palace and rampaged through the city park of Daphne. In helpless rage they stoned the five brass statues of the emperor and his family, ripped them from their pedestals and dragged them through the streets.

The government retaliated swiftly, imposing curfews, martial law and vicious recriminatory measures on the ringleaders and innocent alike. The crisis occasioned the emergence of John Chrysostom, a newly ordained priest and long time scholar of the Bible. He stepped into a leadership vacuum and initiated steps for restoring law and order, pleading with the military to restrain themselves and the people to pull themselves together.

A vivid and dramatic speaker, he captured the terror of the hour in one of his homilies. "Some were executed by the sword, others burned to death, others were thrown to wild beasts. Among these were old people and children. Without the slightest warning they were led to execution. Mothers followed at a distance and saw their son's heads struck off. They did not dare to weep. Their fear was greater than their pain" (Hom. 3).

Fearing more reprisals, Flavian, the Bishop of Antioch decided to go to Constantinople and negotiate a clemency decree from the emperor. Flavian assigned Chrysostom with the task of calming the people and the civil administration until his return. To this purpose Chrysostom employed his considerable speaking talent, beginning a series of sermons on the First Sunday of Lent, since known as the homilies "On the Statues."

Ingeniously combining political commentary and motivation to spiritual renewal, Chrysostom's sermons produced the twofold effect of cooling down the people and increasing their Christian awarenesses. In assigning blame for the riots, Chrysostom accused troublemakers from the foreign elements in Antioch, but he also stated that the sins of the people—their self-indulgence, swearing and blaspheming—were a part of the reason for the civil disorder. Very much the moralizer, Chrysostom reminded them that it should now be clear that the danger and peril they experienced disclosed the transitoriness of wealth, glory and possessions. They must now put their whole trust in God and not set the pagans a bad example by cowardice and despondency. His Lenten sermons won their hearts and launched him on a preaching career that was to earn him the title of "The Golden Mouth."

Bishop Flavian returned just before Easter with a welcome amnesty from the emperor. Chrysostom captured the wild joy of the people in his Easter homily. "Glory be to God, who has given back the head (Bishop Flavian) to the body, the teacher to his pupils. Decorate not only your houses, but also your hearts, and never cease to praise God for his benefits" (Homily 21).

A native son of Antioch, the city in which the followers of Jesus were first called Christians, Chrysostom was born of a Roman father and a Greek mother. His father died soon after his birth and his early education was directed by his mother. He claims that during his adolescent years he was "ensnared by the lusts of the world," enjoying the theater and the other pleasures of the city. He received a classical education, including speaking lessons from Libanius, the most prominent orator of the day.

At the age of eighteen he must have experienced some kind of religious conversion—or heeded the urging of his religious-minded mother—because he terminated his secular pursuits and entered the monastery school of Diodorus for the purpose of studying the Bible. Three years later he joined a commune of monks in the nearby mountains. After four years with them, he intensified his spiritual quest and moved to a cave hermitage. Within two years it became clear to him that his health would never hold up in that asthma-inducing cave, nor under the severe austerities of his self-imposed asceticism.

He came down from his six-year stay in the mountains to the city of his birth. As a trained classicist, biblical scholar and experienced monk, he made an ideal candidate for pastoral ministry in the Antioch Church. He accepted ordination to the deaconate and served in that capacity for five years, at which time Bishop Flavian called him to the priesthood. It was during his first year in the priesthood that he preached the epic sermons about the tax riots mentioned previously.

That turbulent first year of his priesthood was followed by a decade of comparative quiet in which he fulfilled his pastoral duties and preached the hundreds of sermons on the Scriptures. They were listened to with enthusiasm, recorded by secretaries and earned him the title of Doctor of the Church.

At the age of fifty-two, he was named the Bishop-Patriarch of Constantinople, the capitol city of the Eastern empire. In his new appointment he was plunged into controversy, conflict and tensions resulting from religious and political antagonisms.

He found a diocese with a badly managed budget, insufficient services for the poor and the sick, clerical laxity and ostentatious hedonism among the rich. He sold most of the expensive furniture in the Bishop's house and stopped the custom of hosting expensive dinner parties, using the money for social services. He cut back all church expenses and campaigned to raise the social concerns' awareness for the poor among the prosperous.

He fired one deacon for being a murderer and another for being a known adulterer. He put a stop to vagabond monks living undisciplined lives outside of their monasteries and ordered them to go back and live with their communities. More than ever he dwelt on moral themes in his sermons, thundering forth his disgust with the violence and erotic character of the theater and the public games. Dismayed by the pervasive alcoholism and gluttony of his people, he confronted them with their immorality and threatened them with God's judgments.

His acid comments about the theater have a contemporary ring. Berating the males in his congregation, he speaks forthrightly. "What have I long said about the theater? You get off balance when you meet a woman in the street. Then if you see a shameless woman in the theater, flaunting her soft sensuality, singing her immoral songs, throwing her limbs about in the dance, do you dare to say that nothing happens to you? Long after the play, those images will float in your mind. You go home, not alone, but with the whore in your heart, kindling the Babylonian furnace."

Colorfully direct, Chrysostom adds a sanction to his words. "I announce in a loud voice. If any of you goes to the sinful outrages of the theater, I will not allow him back to this Church, nor to approach the Holy Table. I will do as shepherds do, who separate the mangy sheep from the flock, lest they contaminate others" (Quoted by Palladius, 17).

He raged at his clergy for keeping "virgins" and "deaconesses" in their rectories as cooks, when in fact they were really mistresses. He ordered the women to join convents if they wanted vowed, virginal life. Yet despite the severity expressed in these sermons, he was also the forgiving pastor. "If you have fallen a second time, or even a thousand times, come to me and you shall be healed."

His moral vision was culturally biased by the male chauvinism of his day so that he tended to place the woman in the temptress role, whom the male must resist, not adverting to the fact that the male is every bit as capable of doing some aggressive tempting himself.

Political struggles with other bishops, as well as disciplinary measures taken against his own clergy and monks, drew him into a succession of conflicts that eventually caused his downfall and tragic end. He was responsible for deposing six bishops for practicing simony, the buying of ecclesiastical positions. He was outspoken against absentee bishops who ignored their dioceses in favor of living in the imperial city and seeking royal favor at the imperial court. He publicly stated that these bishops should be home taking care of their people. He made an enemy out of the bishop of Alexandria because he would not let the man dominate him and use him for his political purposes.

These various bishops, in alliance with the indolent rich at the court who were much offended by

Chrysostom's forceful criticism of their self-indulgence, campaigned militantly with the emperor Arcadius and the empress Eudoxia to impeach and exile this cranky bishop who was ruining their fun and their "harmless" intrigues.

They took every chance to smear his reputation and mount a hate campaign against him. They unsuccessfully attempted to depose him at the Synod of the Oak, so called for it was held in a monastery in the middle of a park of oak trees. They found their ultimate weapon by misquoting an intemperate sermon he gave against the dedication of a silver statue of the empress which was accompanied by the hedonistic excesses he deplored. This dedication took place outside the cathedral during liturgy. Chyrsostom was preaching about the beheading of John the Baptist. He applied the message to the sacrilege going on outside the cathedral door, dwelling at length on the evil Herodias.

His enemies persauded the empress Eudoxia that he was making a personal attack on her. Slightly changing his words, they implied he meant her when he thundered, "Herodias dances again. Once again she dances for John's head." (It did not seem to matter that it was Salome who did the dancing.) His adversaries convinced Eudoxia, who thereupon ordered Chrysostom exiled to Armenia.

He survived there for three years, still keeping in touch by writing letters and receiving visitors. He was then consigned to exile even further away and died en route. His last words were, "Glory to God for all things."

Reflection

Chrysostom was a moralizer in the best sense of the word, for he sincerely practiced what he preached. He lived in simplicity and poverty, while actively building hospitals and providing services for the poor. He raged against the sins of the rich for the purpose of touching their consciences and changing their values so they might see the needs of the deprived. Perhaps chauvinistically too hard on women, he was clearly just as tough with the sins of male clergy, be they bishops, monks or priests. Moreover, his biblical scholarship and oratorical eloquence raised what could have been tedious moralizing into an art form, so that his homilies continue to be read as models of preaching as well as spiritual inspiration to this day.

Augustine

(354–430)

Above All A Pastor

"Late have I loved Thee, beauty so ancient and so new,
late have I loved thee."

Augustine's Confessions

Augustine came late to the love of Christ, but seldom
has any Christian ever loved Jesus with such fiery
passion as this North African saint. Born in Tagaste,
354, of Monica and Patricius, Augustine was raised as
a Christian, though not a baptized one. His parents
instilled middle-class values in him and fostered a
hunger for education and learning. When he was
sixteen, he was sent by his parents to Carthage to
study law at the university. Augustine's tastes,
however, ran to literature and girls. After several love
affairs, he settled in with one woman with whom he
lived for the next fifteen years and by whom he sired a
son, Adeodatus.

Feeling guilty and uncomfortable about his sex life,
Augustine sought relief from religion. His literary
leanings moved him to study the Bible, but he recoiled
from what appeared to him to be a contradiction
between a vengeful Old Testament God and a loving
New Testament Christ. Moreover the stories seemed
too coarse and unreal for his intellectual tastes that
were nourished by the refinement of the Latin classics.

Augustine then investigated the Manichean religion,
which repudiated the value of the Old Testament. This
religion held a low opinion of the goodness of human

nature and called for a self-disciplined austerity that could one day lead its members to membership in a godly elite. Augustine converted to this religion that seemed to soothe his guilt feelings as well as suit his lifelong ascetic bent which he inherited from his mother.

After ten years of teaching in Carthage, he moved to Rome and opened a school for boys. Within a year influential friends obtained a teaching position for him at the court of the emperor of Milan, then the political capital of the West.

In Milan, three elements combined to move Augustine to seek Christian Baptism: the sermons of Ambrose, the spiritual insights of the Neo-Platonists, and a flash of light from St. Paul's writings. Augustine loved to attend the cathedral services on Sunday morning and was exceptionally impressed with the sermons of Ambrose who cleared away his problems with the Old Testament and made such a challenging appeal for the Catholic faith.

In studying the Neo-Platonists, at the urging of Ambrose, he came to realize the reality of the spiritual. Then one day in his garden, he thought he heard a child call out playfully, "Take and read." He picked up the Epistles of Paul and read from Romans 13, "Let us live decently as people do in the daytime: no drunken orgies, no promiscuity or licentiousness, and no wrangling or jealousy. Let your armor be the Lord Jesus Christ. Forget about satisfying your bodies." In that moment his doubts dissolved and his soul filled with light. He became a Christian and began one of the most brilliant Christian careers ever lived.

Soon after his Baptism, Augustine journeyed back to Africa. His mother died along the way and his son died upon arrival in Africa. He returned to the outskirts of his hometown and founded a small monastery. About one year later, while in Hippo on a recruiting tour for members of his monastery, he attended the liturgy at the local cathedral, where the bishop delivered a sermon urging the people to select a priest for service in the city. The record shows that the people turned to Augustine and elected him. They brought him forward and had the bishop ordain him immediately—a method of election unusual for us, but apparently not uncommon in those days.

Augustine moved his monastery to Hippo and began his celebrated preaching career in the cathedral. The bishop liked Augustine so well that he ordained him as his assistant bishop and successor. The bishop died a few years later and Augustine began a thirty-five year tenure as bishop of Hippo.

Augustine excelled as a pastor, preacher, and nourisher of the faith of his people. Unlike many of the other 300 bishops of Africa who lived conspicuously wealthy lives, Augustine embraced simplicity and poverty, converting the Hippo residence into a monastery. Impressed by the ideal of Christian community described in the Acts of the Apostles, he sought to reproduce the atmosphere of love, prayer, and common sharing that characterized the "Jerusalem Communes" in the days after Pentecost.

The author of the *City of God, The Confessions,* and the *Tract of the Trinity* as well as numerous books assaulting the heresies of the Manicheans, Donatists, and Pelagians, Augustine the pastor/preacher strenuously nourished the faith of his Hippo parishioners for thirty-five years.

As pastor and preacher, Augustine was not physically isolated from his audience by a pulpit or lectern. Today the preacher stands and the people sit. In Hippo the preacher sat and the people stood. His eyes and theirs met, separated only by a few yards. A flood of words flowed from Augustine, infused with excitement so that he might identify with his listeners' need to be moved. He felt a need to be part of his people, to appeal to their feelings for him and to react sensitively to their emotions.

One of his major themes was "The Christian
Struggle." The arena was the heart upon which
occurred a struggle with the forces and desires that
could ruin the person. Victory depends on adherence to
an inner power who is Christ. "When this inner power
sleeps, the boat of the soul is rocked by desires for the
world. When this Christ wakes in the soul, it becomes
calm again."

Augustine realized that convincing his listeners was
not an easy task. His demanding message was like a
river flowing into a system of side streams, thus losing
its power in the minds of his hearers. As he sat there
preaching year after year, he came to recognize how
little he ever really penetrated their hearts, no matter
how often they broke out in cheers at his talks.

He once gave a sermon on Psalm 54, "Darkness has
overwhelmed me. O that I had the wings of the dove,
that I could fly away and be at peace." Then he spoke
of the clouds of sheer anger that gathered in his mind
about the intractable people with whom he must deal—
"warped, misshapen people, committed to my
responsibility. On whom all my zeal and insistence is
spent in vain."

To his credit, he overcame the depression and spoke
more forgivingly and warmly to them whom he had
thought of as "dust and ashes." To his worldly
parishioners he said, "The world is a smiling place.
Small wonder you enjoy it so immoderately. I don't
blame you. I understand." He rarely rebuked the rich
in the strong words that Ambrose would have used.
Augustine worked on healing the tensions between rich
and poor. "Look at the rich man beside you. He has a
lot of money, but may have no avarice, while you who
have no money, may have much avarice."

Though he spoke with great feeling, he never did so
merely to stir up the emotion of his listeners. He
identified strongly with Christ's "feeding of the
multitudes." He would feed his people with the Word of
God, as Christ fed the hungry people who followed him

into the desert with the multiplication of the loaves. As a teenager he had stolen some pears to supply his friends with a few tidbits; now he would "pirate" the Bible for food for his people. He told Jerome that he could never be a detached Bible scholar, "If I gain any knowledge from the Bible, I pay it out immediately to my people." He was driven to speak to them with the utmost power and regretted he, of all people, could not live up to his own ideals of communication. "I am saddened that my tongue cannot live up to my heart."

He found time to give pastoral care despite a workload that would daunt any modern executive. He acted as a judge in the bishop's court where he arbitrated endless cases. He counseled his priests, administered the property of the diocese, and joined with other African bishops in the great Councils of the day. He carried on a huge correspondence with friends and acquaintances and wrote countless treatises, composing thirty books alone between 395 and 410.

During the final years of his life, Augustine witnessed the stages in the decline and fall of the Roman empire, beginning with the sack of Rome in 410. As he neared his death, he lamented the invasion of North Africa by the Vandals and he grieved over the stories of the burning of churches, the torturing of ascetics, the raping of virgins, and the slaughtering of bishops and priests. He did his best to console the refugees who packed into Hippo.

When the final weeks of his own life seemed sure, he ordered someone to write out the four psalms of David dealing with penance and to place them on his bedroom walls where he could see them and meditate on them constantly. Throughout his last ten days, he forbade visitors except at meal times and when the doctor would come, for he wanted time for meditation.

Augustine died and was buried on August 28, 430.

Reflection

It is well known that Augustine is one of the most influential theologians of Catholic Church history. His thought literally dominated theology for a thousand years after his death, and his writings are still widely read throughout the Christian world. Yet he was not the theologian-scholar in the modern sense, a man seldom in contact with parish people, or rarely able to communicate the Gospel to ordinary people.

Augustine's great genius was to be ever the pastoral theologian, even though he was capable of high flights of abstract speculation, as in the case of his tract on the Trinity. What makes his writings so universally appealing is partly due to his refusal to flinch from controversy and partly attributable to his fidelity to the pastoral care of his people in Hippo.

When *Time* magazine (Dec. 31, 1979) chose the current seven greatest preachers in the United States, it selected only parish men: "Only preachers who nurture a congregation week by week, year after year, were considered, thus ruling out Billy Graham and the TV personalities. Those chosen had to convey, along with solid content and skillful delivery, the sense of overwhelming conviction that is one of the golden keys to great preaching."

In retrospect it seems that for many people this is the most attractive feature of the ministry of Augustine. We may admire his mighty religious thoughts, but perhaps we should be in greater awe of the fact that so much of that thinking was germinated in the "basilica pacis" where he sat so many hours with his people and counseled their souls and hearts about Christ. His human appeal and pastoral devotion remain the best testimony to his meaning for the Church.

Monica

(332–387)

A Mighty Mother

"My mother sang with joy a hymn of Ambrose about
the Trinity. Then she said, 'There you have beyond all
question the happy life.' "

Confessions *9, 22*

In his Confessions Augustine portrays his mother as
a genuinely attractive woman, possessing qualities he
would like in himself as bishop—restrained, dignified,
beyond gossip, and a calming influence on her friends
and acquaintances. He presents an idealized memory
of Monica, raised in a Christian family, devoted to the
traditional piety of the African Church such as keeping
the fast on Saturdays and bringing meal offerings to
the tombs of the dead.

She does not emerge in his description as a naive or
simple soul, for she is every bit as insistent as her
husband Patricius that Augustine should have a good
classical education. She saw no conflict between such
a "pagan" education and the Christian character
development of her son, but seemed really to believe it
would contribute to making him a better Christian.

Monica does not escape the particular leanings
common to the African Church of her day. The African
Christians eagerly sought ecstatic experiences by
drunkenness, chanting and wild dances. At the age of
six, she was on the way to being too fond of wine until
her pride was wounded by being accused of "tippling
too much." In sheer stubbornness she determined never
to let that happen to her again.

While she does not seem to have joined in chants and dances that brought on a kind of religious trance, she did put great stock in dreams. Her people believed that dreams were direct glimpses of another world, a world which literally invaded this one through the dreams one had while asleep. She found it quite easy to consult her dreams and to trust them when they told her about the future of her son and she believed she knew how to tell which of those dreams was authentic.

A case in point may be seen when we review her reaction to her son's becoming a Manichean and taking in a mistress. She was furious about this turn of events and refused to let him live at home and eat at her table while she thus would have to put up with his "blasphemies" as she called them. She relented as a result of a consoling dream in which she met a "radiant being" who questioned her about her grief. She told him she was worrying about her son. The being assured her she had little to fear, adding "Your son is with you."

She welcomed her son home and told him about the dream. Augustine dismissed the dream by saying that he and his mother would get along much better if she would convert to his new religion. Firm as always she replied, "He did not say I was with you, but that you were with me."

Clearly a woman of formidable inner strength, she spoke and acted with such certitude that she generally unnerved anyone attempting to resist her. There is no question that the stories that survive about Monica present her as a "tough woman," almost relentless in some respects. A lighter comment could soften the picture by comparing her to the ever present and over solicitous "Jewish Mother" in contemporary imagery. As Augustine puts it, "She loved to have me with her, as is the way with all mothers, but far more than most mothers."

She did indeed want to be with him even in his adult years, and was willing to cross land and sea to do so.

When Augustine decided to go to Rome and seek his fortune there, Monica traveled to the ship, bought a ticket and planned to go right along. Augustine did not want her trailing him around, so he resorted to a trick to evade her. He told her he was going to spend the night with a friend. That night, while she innocently passed the hours in prayer for her son's conversion, he boarded a night passage and went off without her. This twenty-eight-year-old man was ashamed of doing this to his mother, and still had a residue of remorse years later when he wrote the story in his Confessions. "Thus I lied to my mother—and such a mother!"

She could be just as forceful with her husband. It was common enough for African husbands of that period to beat their wives, but Patricius never laid a hand on Monica. She had taken the measure of her husband and knew how to control him. She told her friends, with some hint of sarcasm, that "They were after all 'slave girls' of their husbands. It was not for them 'to rise up against their lord and master.' " She had no intention of being a battered wife.

She did not revolt; she simply used a successful passive-aggressive stance that seemed to work well. When he was angry about something, she knew how to wait out the storm, and not provoke him while he was mad. But, when he cooled down, she resolutely explained how she had been right in the first place. She disapproved of his infidelities and his paganism. Again she waited him out, not in total passivity, for it was ever her intention to make him faithful and convert him to Christianity. She won both battles.

Augustine frequently comments on his mother's capacity for prayers and tears. One may account for the tears as a culturally approved emotional outlet of an African woman. But her prayers grew out of a faith in Christ and a confidence in the divine power that we can expect to find in a saint, and hope to find in all Christians, whether canonized or not. Monica believed in the faith that could move mountains, even so redoubtable a one as her son. The intensity of her human concentration on desired goals matched, and certainly supplemented, her single-minded piety with its persistent prayer and regular fasting. In retrospect Augustine never doubted that his mother's prayers had much to do with his ultimate conversion.

Stranded at an African dockside, angry and frustrated by her son's behavior, Monica let none of this hold her back. She simply boarded a ship and followed him to Rome, but by the time she found out where he might be there, he had journeyed further to Milan. On she traveled after him to that imperial city. Much to her surprise and delight, she found a changed son. Augustine had grown disillusioned with Manicheism for various reasons, a prominent one being the persuasive sermons of the cultivated Ambrose, Bishop of Milan.

Augustine declared to his mother that he was taking instructions to become a Christian. The overjoyed mother could not have been aware then that this was a delaying tactic on the part of Augustine. He knew there was little chance of escaping her, but he could quiet her down and please her with this news about entering the catechumenate. In his mind of course, it could take years before he would actually accept baptism, if ever. And that was his mood of the moment.

Monica realized immediately that Ambrose was part of the reason for the good news. Augustine comments, "She hastened to Church more zealously than ever and drank in the words of Ambrose as a fountain of water. . . . She loved that man as an angel of God." And ever the arranger, she set about to find a rich wife for her son, having forced him to give up his mistress.

Three years pass in which Augustine establishes his reputation as a renowned thinker and obtains a well paid position as a teacher. It is near the end of this period that he experiences his true conversion to Christ. When he tells Monica, she becomes jubilant with triumph. No one could be happier than she to see the conversion for which she had prayed and yearned for so long. Augustine wrote, "She praised You, O God, who are powerful enough, and more than powerful enough to carry out your purpose beyond all hopes and dreams."

Simultaneous with his conversion, Augustine comes down with a severe asthma attack. Fortunately, the vacation time for teachers was just beginning, so Augustine, Monica, his son, his brother and two cousins retired to a country villa in Cassiciacum. This was a chance for Augustine to rebuild his health as well as to prepare for Baptism and spend some time in creative leisure.

Predictably, Monica takes charge of the household. Cooking, presiding, "needling," she is a strong presence in this unlikely group of "philosophers," composed of a pious old lady, two uneducated cousins, and two private pupils aged sixteen. The record of their dialogues reveals the artistry of an Augustine as a teacher who is able to draw from the group the capacity to perform beyond their normal selves.

Monica breaks in on their dialogue one day and asks about their progress. Augustine told the secretary to note her question and she said, "What are you doing? I thought women were not allowed to be part of such a discussion." Augustine answered, "Mother, you know the meaning of the Greek term philosophy, namely, love of wisdom." He goes on to tell her that she is the greatest lover of wisdom he has ever met. Just as nimbly she replied, "I have never known you to tell an untruth before."

After the baptism of Augustine, he and his mother, brother and son began the trip home to Africa. Arriving at the port of Ostia, they were forced to halt their trip due to a naval blockade. During their stay,

Monica became mortally ill. For the last nine days of her life she was totally withdrawn, and opened up only near the end to bless her sons and to tell Augustine she had never heard one sharp word from him and secondly that she no longer cared that she would not be buried by her husband.

Augustine closed her eyes and made arrangements for the funeral. Though he was deeply grieved he shed no tears at first, but finally "found solace in weeping." In commenting on the need to cry he argued to himself that it was the way to heal the "wound of loss."

Reflection

It is due to Augustine's literary genius that we have such unusual access to the inner life of Monica and quality of her relationships. Some commentators, influenced by contemporary Freudian analysis, tend to classify Monica as the devouring mother, but thereby discount the mysterious workings of faith and grace in her attitude toward her son. They judge her persistence purely in behavioral scientific terms, permitting no room for the dynamics of divine power.

One cannot deny that she seemed to possess some of the qualities of a domineering mother, but no relationship can ever be so easily reduced to one category. Moreover, we have the testimony of Augustine about her deeply spiritual nature, in which he attributes to her the faith that finally brought him to believe in Christ and find a divine love that was not to be compared to any he had ever known.

He knew his mother was a saint.

So do we.

Patrick

(389–461)

A Roman Converts the Irish

"In my dreams I heard the voices of the Irish. 'We beg
you, come and walk among us again.' My heart was
moved."

Patrick's Confessions

Patrick had every reason to hate the Irish. Son of a
Roman family living in West Britain, he was taught to
feel superior to the people living on that island to the
West of his homeland. In addition, at sixteen he was
carried off into slavery in Ireland, remaining there six
years. At the very time of his life when he was
emerging into manhood and preparing a career for
himself, he was deprived of his human rights and
forced into a lonely and humiliating life as a slave to
an Irish farmer.

Everything in Ireland militated against his Roman
training and upbringing. Their tribal and nomadic
ways ran contrary to the stable and orderly
background familiar to him. Instinctively an urban
man, he found himself repelled by immersion in a
primitive agrarian world. Nourished by an enlightened
Christianity, he drew back in distaste from the
prevalent superstitions of the Irish people and the
nature cults of the Druid religion.

It is not clear as to whether he was cruelly treated
by his master, but it is evident that he was personally
offended by the loss of his freedom. He did not like the
Irish and determined to escape them. At the age of
twenty-two, he ran away from the farm and made for

the coast, where he hid until he could find a departing ship. He lucked upon a small ship transporting a pack of hunting dogs to the continent. The crew appears to have been German, and they had pirated these dogs from settlements along the coast, planning to market them back home. Patrick hired himself out as a caretaker of the kennels aboard ship.

They rode through a fearful storm across the channel to the coast of Gaul (France). From there Patrick managed to get back to Britain and the welcome fireside of his home. Prior to his slavery days he showed little sign of being especially religious, but the years of isolation seemed to release a meditative capacity in him.

He decided to study for the priesthood and enrolled in the seminary at Lerins in the north of France. After ordination he served in the diocese of Auxerre for about fifteen years. In planning sessions, Church leaders were beginning to discuss the possibilities of evangelizing Ireland. Patrick was a natural candidate for such an enterprise since he could speak Gaelic and was familiar with Irish life.

We have no record of how Patrick responded at first to this call. The best we can assume is that he may have argued against the appointment, given his unhappy experience in Ireland. In his Confessions he attributes his change of heart to a dream. "In my dream came the voices of the Irish. 'We beg you, come and walk among us again.' My heart was moved. And on another night, whether within me or at my side, I could not tell, God knows, I heard the words, 'He who laid down his life for you. He it is who speaks in you.' "

So Patrick accepted the Irish mission and was ordained a bishop at the age of forty-two. He arrived in Ireland with a small group of missionaries and began a successful effort to root Christianity among the Irish people. Unlike most missionaries to alien cultures who acquire on-site identity with the local culture after seminary training, Patrick comes with a ready-made understanding of the people, and a mastery of their language, all the more effective since this was obtained during the impressionable years of his youth. Patrick reversed that normal missionary procedure by knowing the people first and then going to the seminary, and, in addition, having accomplished fifteen years of parish ministry before becoming a missionary. This lengthy and unusually broad preparation may well account for the remarkable effectiveness of his Irish mission.

The Ireland of that period was tribal, divided into a series of clans, each presided over by a chief or "king." Part of Patrick's strategy was to convert the head of a clan because then the likelihood of the other members of the clan converting was more assured. In particular he aimed at converting the head of the most powerful clan in Ireland at that time, namely, the one at Tara.

The only record we have of his meeting with the clan chief, his wife, lieutenants and Druidic priests at Tara is in a colorful legend in which Patrick and the Druids engage in magical combat, and the Druids lose. It seems reasonable to conclude that the meeting was far more one of confrontation at the start, and not one of pleasant, friendly ecumenical dialogue.

One thing is certain, Patrick had a lot going for him in the sense that he knew the language of the Irish. He was fully aware of the etiquette and protocol of clan behavior and was bright enough to work off from the deficiencies and weaknesses of the nature cults. He could talk and act like an Irishman, but with a Roman accent, and that alone would intrigue the clan leader. He showed respect for their customs and their culture to the point where he could plead for a respectful hearing of his case for Christianity.

At the same time he carried in his person an aura of power, for he was a Roman, son of an army officer and bishop of his Church. In other words he entered into negotiations with the "king" of Tara from a position of strength—personal, cultural and official. Add to this the depth of Christian faith residing in the heart of one of the great missionaries of Church history and one can appreciate why he had a good chance of prevailing at Tara. However the conversion happened, or how long it took, the fact is that it did occur, thus providing the Church with a firm foothold in Ireland.

Patrick realized he was not dealing with total barbarians as he was taught to believe during his youth. For example, in the area of law Patrick discovered that the Irish had created a sophisticated system of civil law, known as the "Brehon Law" every bit as engaging in its subtlety as the Roman Law with which he was familiar. Having one time considered being a lawyer, he knew sound law when he saw it. Though the Irish were mainly an oral culture, transmitting their history through the memorized poem-songs of the bards, they also possessed an alphabet and inscribed whatever they preferred to write on stones rather than book paper.

As a Roman, Patrick was taught to admire art in its architectural forms. The Irish of his time had little taste for marble halls, living rather in plain wooden or straw homes, but they were master artists in the making of gold ornaments, and shrewd craftsmen in the creating of metal weapons and utensils. But then as now, the true gift of the Irish was poetry that grew from a literary imagination unparalleled for the times. In Patrick's time they were creating the first great saga in any vernacular language, a saga that was to provide the basic themes for the literature of England and other neighboring nations.

It is true that Patrick still thought of them as barbarians when it came to their living conditions, so primitive when compared to the Roman towns with stone and marble homes, paved roads, water systems and public baths.

The important thing to remember is that Patrick had overcome whatever negative feelings he had about their culture and identified with the people. What is more to the point, he put the control of the Church in their hands and permitted it to develop as a genuinely Irish Church.

Patrick was insightful enough to know that the Roman style of the Church with which he was familiar, with its orderly dioceses and parishes and with its chain of command from bishop to priest to people very much depended on a Roman cultural base. Patrick permitted the Irish Church to think through in their own due time the connection between their moral behavior and the gospel teachings of Christ as well as finding their own administrative style more in accord with the clan system.

Patrick's missionary method took into account the importance of culture, customs and traditions in determining the self-respect and identity of a people. His sensitivity probably accounts for the fact that the conversion of Ireland was the most peaceful in the history of missionary effort in the sense that there were no martyrs during the process of conversion. It is true there was opposition, sometimes violent, but never to the point of death.

Patrick ministered for about thirty years in Ireland. By the time of his death Christianity had been sufficiently established so that the process of evangelizing the whole people could proceed successfully in the years to come. Our official sources for his life are found in two of his writings, *The Confessions,* in which he described and explained his mission work, and "The Letter to the Soldiers of Coroticus," wherein he condemned the Welsh Christian soldiers for raiding the Irish coast and killing Irish Christians.

He died on March 17.

The Irish have never forgotten him or that date.

Reflection

We noted at the beginning of this essay that Patrick had every reason to dislike the Irish. At the end of his life he could think of no reason to stop loving them. He identified so closely with the people of Ireland that most people today simply take it for granted that he must have been Irish. He conquered them with his Christian religion. They won his heart so firmly that in the end he seemed to be one of them. What should have been, in human terms, a notorious mis-match turned out to have been, if one may say it a "union made in heaven."

In the year that Patrick died, the Church in Rome was struggling for its life in an empire that was collapsing. But far to the north it was born again. The evangelized would become the evangelizer.

Columban

(543?–615)

Monk and Missionary

"We are chained to the Chair of St. Peter. Holy Father,
look after the peace of the Church. Stand between your
sheep and the wolves."

Columban's letter to Boniface IV

The fall of the Roman Empire (c. 476) put a severe
strain on the existence of Christianity, especially in
Europe north of the Alps. The triumph of the Gothic
warriors marked the end of Roman political influence,
with its urban emphasis, and signaled a reversion to
countryside rural living for the ruling class. While
some of the top leadership embraced the Christian
faith in the Franco-Germanic lands, the peasantry
remained pagan.

The Church needed some effective system for
converting the seminomadic peasants. The answer
turned out to be monasticism. Martin of Tours (397)
had already initiated a monastic mission to rural
France. Patrick brought this monastic ideal to Ireland
around 461. Out of this seedbed of Irish monasticism
emerged the dominant missionary effort of the Church
to the Europe of the sixth and seventh centuries. The
Irish monks were the groundbreakers in this work of
reconstructing Christianity and the Benedictine monks
were to come after them as the stabilizers of what the
Irish monks had started. And behind it all stands the
figure of Pope Gregory the Great, like a Napoleonic
commander, setting forth a policy and direction for the
completion of the conversion of Europe.

We will first treat the story of Columban and the Irish monks in this chapter and then take the story of Benedict and the Roman monks in the next chapter.

An appreciation of Columban and Irish monasticism requires some understanding of the shape of the Irish Church of that time. As has been mentioned, Patrick adapted the faith to the cultural patterns of the people whose social system was that of the clan. The Ireland of that period was totally rural. There were no cities, nor any system of roads connecting all parts of the country as would be the case in a Roman territory.

The Roman Church normally had a diocesan administrative approach that was based on an existing urban model. Bishops served as the ecclesiastical counterparts of the urban government officials. But in Ireland the administrative model was that of the clan, an intensely communal gathering ruled by the chief, completely rural and partly nomadic. For this reason, monasticism, as it was imported by Patrick from France, became the administrative model for the Irish.

Monks thrived in a farmers world. Monks lived together in communes just as did the clans. Monks had abbot leaders like the clan chiefs. Here was a social system completely congenial to the Irish temperament and one which they adopted wholeheartedly. Abbots and Abbesses ruled the Irish Church. Some men in each monastery were ordained either as bishops or priests for sacramental purposes only. Sometimes the abbot was a bishop, most times he was a layman.

Many of these Irish monastic settlements soon became centers of learning, scholarship and art. Many more concentrated on ideals of asceticism. It was from the "ascetic" monasteries that the Irish missionaries came—but not for missionary reasons. The Irish monks who flowed to Iona and Scotland and the European territories did so for ascetic reasons. Like Abraham of the Bible, cutting ties with their homeland, and in the spirit of the Gospel, they took Christ's words about "leaving father, mother and family" literally and went to live in a strange land.

Once in these new lands, they discovered a new call, namely, to convert the local peasantry to Christ. They became missionaries by coincidence more than by intention.

This kind of world bred the Columban of this story. As a young man he joined the "scholar" monastery of Clonard, where the study of the Latin Bible and certain Latin authors constituted a major part of the curriculum. Columban liked his studies but was battling to keep his vow of celibacy intact. He was attracted to women, and they to him. It is most likely there would have been women students at Clonard as this was common enough at some monastery schools of this period. Possibly it was a "double" monastery, that is, one of monks and nuns, with the government of the whole community held jointly by an abbess and an abbot-bishop, like that of St. Brigid's foundation at Kildare.

Whatever the reason for Columban's celibacy difficulties, he decided to solve his problem by transferring to an "ascetic" monastery at Bangor, the strictest of all the religious houses of Ireland. Here he encountered and accepted the stern discipline that he and other monks would export to the continent. He would also learn the "penitentials," an examination of conscience related to the custom of private confession developing in the Irish Church.

After some years of training he was ready to take the final step in ascetic renunciation. He had already left his family setting in the southeast of Ireland, now he would leave the country itself as a sign of his total commitment to Christ. He would break all emotional ties to his homeland so that his personal life could belong exclusively to the Lord.

Setting out with twelve companions, he sailed for France. Wearing his monk's tunic and carrying a leather bag containing a copy of the Bible, he and his friends severed their roots and traveled to a different country. They came upon a land where Christianity wás practically unknown in the countryside and not all that well practiced in the devastated urban centers. Since they could speak Latin they met no language barriers with the leadership classes, but they would need to learn the romance dialects of the old peasantry and the odd Gothic tongue of the new.

Since their natural habitat was a rural one, they soon settled into a remote farm area called Luxeuil, the site of a ruined fort. Columban framed a strict Rule for this foundation and the hundred or so monasteries that were to owe their origin, at least indirectly, to Luxeuil. Far more severe than that of Benedict, Columban's Rule exacted absolute obedience to the Abbot. It commanded as much silence as possible. It reduced food to a minimum and called for the monks to get up before they had slept sufficiently. It contained a list of sins and a set of penalties much tougher than that of the Benedictine Rule.

On the other hand Columban's monasteries became the center of agrarian reform. He and his monks cleared the forests and put back into cultivation much of the land that had been desolated by the Gothic-Roman wars. He replaced the scorched earth policy of wartime with the restoration of the fertility of the earth. The monasteries of Columban's farmer monks were laying the groundwork for the economic rebirth of Europe by creating a standard and stabilized food supply for the people. His monks not only created these monastic farms, but also taught the peasantry how to produce farms of their own. Columban's monasteries became the agricultural schools of northern Europe.

At the same time Columban and his monks patiently remolded the pagan religion of the peasants into a Christian faith. They did not attack pagan customs, but ingeniously crowded it out by what we would call today a kind of behavior modification or substitute association. They permitted the people to continue

reverencing the sacred stones and wells but gradually
changed the conscious associations from nature deities
to Christian saints and to Christ. In this Columban and
his followers emulated the missionary technique of
Patrick in his adaptation of Christianity to Ireland. On
the continent Columban found his totally ascetic
haven. He also discovered that his career was to be a
missionary.

The bishops and kings were pleased with Columban's
Christianizing efforts and his farm improvements. They
were not at all happy with other aspects of his
behavior and that of his monks. Bishops disliked the
fact that he treated them as house chaplains rather
than Church superiors. They were also offended that
his monasteries celebrated Easter at a different date
from themselves. Mainly they were angry that they had
no control over Columban and his monasteries. Nor
would he allow it. Thoroughly imbued with the Irish
custom of Abbot as chief administrator, he saw no
reason to change. Moreover, in many cases he had
little respect for what he perceived to be the softness of
bishops' lifestyle.

The kings turned against him when he started
criticizing their immorality. Columban, the fiery ascetic
from Bangor, the man who had struggled with his
celibacy at Clonard, the enforcer of the penitentials in
his monasteries, had little patience with the easygoing
morals of the royal courts. Nor was he given to tact
and diplomacy in telling them about their sins.
Probably a Celtic hot-head and surely an ascetic
burning with ideals of moral purity, Columban bluntly
confronted the mighty with their wayward morals.

The bishops tried to get Pope Gregory to suppress
Columban and did not succeed. The king of the area,
where Luxeuil existed, did succeed—in a way.

He threw Columban out of the country, putting him
on a boat returning to Ireland. But the stormy sea
threw the boat back to the coast of France.

Irrepressible as ever, Columban disembarked, went on a preaching tour across France and then turned his attention to Switzerland. He founded a monastic settlement at Lake Constance, and left it in the hands of a brother monk, Gall, after whom the monastery was eventually named.

Still the restless man, he went to Italy where he met a friendly king who gave him land in the Apennine mountains in a valley called Bobbio. Here Columban established St. Peter's Monastery and culminated his career as monk, agriculturalist and moralist, and spiritual father of over one hundred monasteries.

Within a century practically all Columban's monasteries adopted the more moderate Rule of St. Benedict. The abbots eventually conceded the administrative supremacy of the bishops, but did retain a large measure of independence, especially for internal matters. The "Columban Monasteries" acted as pioneers in a difficult missionary effort. The Benedictine replacements followed through with less austere lifestyles and the capacity to stabilize and continue the gains made. Europe and the Church benefited well from both groups of monks.

Reflection

While the details of Columban's life remain shrouded in the mythical lore commonly reserved in the sixth and seventh centuries for outstanding leaders, one can move tentatively back to the man through the works he accomplished. The sheer physical drive of the man in moving so widely over different parts of the continent, climbing over the Alps in his old age and determined always to root his vision in yet another new monastery still dazzles us. But more than the physical energy is the spiritual power he permitted to flow through him. That is a major talent of all saints. And one we seek to nourish ourselves.

Benedict

(480?–543)

A Genius for Moderation and Organization

"Prefer nothing to the love of Christ. Hold nothing
dearer than Christ."

Rule of Benedict, IV, V

One of the keys to the success of Benedict, in
contrast to other founders of monasticism, was his
Latin genius for organization. A Roman sense of order
was bred into his bones. Born of a ruling family in the
city of Nursia, central Italy, Benedict assimilated the
Roman administrative know-how with its capacity to
make a practical blend of principle and practice.

In retrospect this seems all the more remarkable
given the fact that Benedict's homeland was an
administrative shambles, reeling under the chaotic
conditions caused by the Gothic invasions and
conquests. He was not seeing first-class models of
practical leadership in the Gothic rulers, but he was
almost certainly tutored in the right method by his
family and the traditions they would wish to preserve
despite their helplessness in the face of the occupation
troops.

His family sent him to Rome for his education. We
do not know how long he stayed in Rome, but only that
when he left the city he did so out of dislike for the life
there. He spent some time in the quiet village of
Enfide, about thirty miles from Rome, where he

appears to have experienced the call to be a monk. The ideal of the monk, as it was then understood, was to "flee the world in order to be alone with God."

Monks had been around for two centuries before Benedict, some of them living in severe isolation as hermits in desolate places, others banding together in austere communities in out-of-the-way places. The "world" which they were fleeing was mainly the hedonistic and chaotic cities of the Roman Empire, though in the case of the Irish monks, especially the "ascetic" ones, this meant simply withdrawal from family and homeland.

Benedict began as a hermit in a cave at a place called Subiaco on property once belonging to Nero. He attracted a few followers, among whom were Maurus and Placidus, sons of Roman senatorial families. Eventually a community of monks asked him to serve as their abbot, but this did not work out well since Benedict was too strict for them. Placidus and Maurus gave him the idea of forming his own community according to his own ideals. Benedict agreed and set up a commune of small huts for his little group. The Subiaco commune experienced a series of harassments from a hostile local cleric, so as a result they decided to move elsewhere.

Benedict selected the site of an abandoned pagan temple on the top of Monte Cassino, where he and his followers constructed a building large enough to house the whole group. The mental and spiritual evolution of Benedict came to maturity at Monte Cassino. The progression from hermitage, to a collection of hermitages, to a unified monastic community, fulfilled the concept of what he seemed called to do and which was taking visible shape at Monte Cassino. This was the "laboratory" where he worked out the final ideas of what he thought monastic life should be. Neither traveler nor missionary, nor especially moved to create a chain of monasteries (he probably is only personally responsible for one other abbey, Terracina), he devoted the full force of his creative genius to producing a model of monastic living at Monte Cassino that served as a pattern for development.

Now Benedict could begin to crystallize the many useful experiences of his life. He had been a hermit, an unsuccessful abbot and an effective leader of the Subiaco commune. He had known chaos in Rome and serenity in the family household at Nursia. In the midst of his final major project to organize life at Monte Cassino, he began composing a landmark document that would prove to be the catalyst for the emergence of the most influential Order in the history of the Church—the Benedictines.

That document is the Rule of St. Benedict.

Without exception, all analyzers of this Rule praise it for its practical combination of principle and its application to the ever changing situations of life. They note its tone of moderation that leaves room for the challenge to the heights of holiness while consoling those who are slowly moving through the stages of spiritual development. Evaluators of the Rule admire the spirit of understanding forgiveness that permeates its philosophy. Virtually all readers of the Rule come away with the relaxing impression that here is a way of life that abhors extremes while creating the possibilities for heroic saintliness.

At the heart of Benedict's Rule is the absolute call to search for God in Christ. Uncompromising in this goal, the Rule goes on to allow for human weakness and frailty in many ways. The Rule does not put people on a treadmill of spiritual growth, insisting on relentless progress through all the desired steps. Instead it is a series of directives, shrewdly devised to accommodate to the endless diversity of human beings.

Fasting is recommended, but not to the point where it will ruin one's health. Prayer is fine, but not to the extent where the work of the monastery is ignored. Faults are to be confronted and corrected, but not in a manner that corners the monk. Rather let the procedure be sufficiently gradual so that the monk has his own part to play in his self-improvement. And always the practicality is permeated with the spiritual goal of union with God through the imitation of Christ, and the power of his grace as manifested in the dynamic presence of the Holy Spirit. Benedict is absolute on this point. If anyone wants to join the monks, it is the duty of those admitting such a person to determine whether or not he has come *to find God.* (Rule LVIII)

The method for finding God would include prayer, fasting, communal living and work—usually farm work. It is Benedict who is famous for the expression that "working can be praying—not just mere working." (Laborare est orare. To work is to pray.)

Benedict died in 543. Benedict left behind him an influential monastery at Monte Cassino and a Rule that needed someone to give it widespread coverage and usage. That person turned out to be Pope Gregory the Great who assumed the Petrine Ministry in 590.

While Pope Gregory may have admired the missionary work of Columban and the Irish monks, he was not pleased with their resistance to the control of bishops, nor did he believe strongly in their extremely austere way of life. The moderateness of the Benedictine Rule appealed to him. So also did the fact that the Benedictines would support the traditional Roman way of ruling the Church.

It was Gregory who encouraged the Benedictine Order to move northwards beyond the Alps and participate in the evangelization of those territories. It was he who sent the Benedictine Augustine to England to supervise the conversion of the Angles who had invaded the country. The backing of so formidable an administrator as Pope Gregory the Great assured the ultimate victory of the Benedictine concept of monasticism in continental Europe, and the consequent decline of the Celtic monasticism.

By the eighth century most of the Columban monasteries on the continent and a majority of Irish foundations in England and Wales adopted the Benedictine Rule. The distinctive style of the Irish Church and its monastic foundations in Ireland was to remain fairly intact until the Norman invasions of the eleventh century, at which time the Roman diocesan system began to prevail.

The Benedictines, however, continued to evangelize the rural peasantry, as did the Columban monks, and to assist with the agricultural improvement of the lands. They pushed into new frontiers and drained swamps and turned many a piece of wretched land into a golden meadow.

They also instituted monastic schools to further the possibilities of education, as well as establishing copying centers for the reproduction of books. All done by hand, these bibles, writings of the Fathers of the Church and classical authors served as the major resources of learning for many generations and insured the preservation of the thinking of the Greek and Roman cultures for the future.

In many instances these Benedictine monasteries became the centers of new towns and cities, as is still demonstrated in the names of places in England by the term "minister" or monastery, for example, Westminster, Yorkminster, and so forth. Hence many of these monasteries evolved into centers for commerce and culture as well as for agriculture. Benedict had created a Rule to help men flee the world to find God. They surely were successful in finding God, as their list of saints and holy men attest. They were also hugely competent as managers and educators, with the result that the world which they fled came to live at their doorsteps.

In the final analysis, it was the monks—Columban and Benedictine—who were the footsoldiers in reconstructing Christianity and expanding its borders in the Europe devastated by the Gothic invasions. To a large extent they midwived the Church through what some historians refer to as the "Dark Ages" of European history. The impulsive drive of a Columban and the serene orderliness of a Benedict, both wedded to an indisputable love of Christ, provided the impetus that was needed. The vision of a Gregory the Great set in motion the explicit missionary policy that claimed Europe for the Church for the next thousand years. Such a triumphant vision, of course, should be modified by the comment that the greater achievement was making available the saving grace and forgiveness of Christ for countless numbers of human beings.

Reflection

One of the astonishing facts about some of these great figures of Church history is that we know so few facts about them. Men such as Patrick, Columban and Benedict, whose influence was clearly immense, remain very much shielded from our view. Former American presidents today fill libraries with the records of their careers, even to the point of retaining a record of all their telephone calls. It would take thousands of hours to read all the historical details associated with Harry Truman. In less than ten minutes we can cover all the known facts about Patrick, Benedict and Columban.

Their lives may not have been committed to the written page, but their effectiveness has been recorded in the faith of millions. We need not resort to myth and legend to satisfy our curiosity about these saints. The record of their spiritual legacy tells us more than enough about them. The impact of their lives seems enough for us. Such is ultimately the case with anyone's life.

Norbert

(1080–1134)

A Builder of Priest Communities

"O priest, your office is not meant for your personal use. You are meant to be a minister of Christ and servant of the people."

Norbert, Ordination Homily

The eleventh-century Church was the kind of world where Luther might have felt at home, for it was a Church teeming with reforms. Pope Gregory VII (Hildebrand) set about eliminating the practice of lay investiture, or lay control of the appointment of bishops. Bernard of Clairvaux and the Cistercians were revolutionizing the monastic world with a stern return to the primitive Rule of Benedict. And Norbert of Xanten led a thoroughgoing movement to improve the lives of the parish clergy. With the Pope focusing on the bishops, Bernard concentrating on the monks and Norbert emphasizing the parish clergy, the times witnessed a resurgence of Christian spirit beneficial to Church and world alike.

Norbert of Xanten, a town near the Holland-German border, did not begin his career as a reformer. Quite the opposite, for he seemed bent on being a clerical opportunist of the type that was actually eroding the credibility and effectiveness of the Church. Through the influence of his family he obtained a financial subsidy from the parish church at Xanten when he accepted ordination to the subdeaconate. His only task was to chant the Divine Office at the Church, but he apparently paid someone a small fee to take his place in the choir, because he gained an appointment as a chaplain—religious counselor to the emperor, Henry V in Cologne.

The salaries from the Xanten fund and the royal treasury were enough to equip him to live in the pleasurable style of the nobility of the times. He was not, however, a man devoid of idealism and moral sensitivity. The seeds of his moral conversion were planted during a lengthy stay in Rome with Henry V in which he witnessed the breakdown of negotiations over the lay-investiture issue. He saw the Pope standing firm on the principle that it was wrong for a secular power to control the appointment of bishops, both because it gave the impression that origin of sacramental ministry comes from a secular source and not from God, and secondly because it contributed to the corruption of the episcopacy. At the same time he noted the emperor would not yield and was willing to keep the Pope under house arrest until the Pope changed his mind.

Norbert found himself sympathetic to the Pope and experiencing the dawn of a moral awakening. This development was accentuated a year later when he was nearly killed by a bolt of lightning during a storm. He decided to withdraw from imperial service and go into seclusion at the abbey of Siburg to permit himself a thorough self-evaluation. After three years of self-scrutiny and prayer, he concluded that he should seek ordination to the priesthood and commit himself to Jesus and the ideals of the Gospel.

A changed man, he returned to the parish community at Xanten, determined to live as a principled priest and anxious to engage in active ministry in the area. The easygoing clergymen of Xanten disliked the "new" Norbert and were annoyed by his enthusiasm as well as by the implied reproach which his life cast on theirs. Realizing that he was out of place with these men, he decided to leave them and embark on a life of evangelical poverty. He divested himself of all his possessions and successfully sought permission from the Pope to become a missionary preacher.

For the next several years he roamed through France preaching repentance and peace and moral reform. The darker side of feudalism gave him much to preach about. The absence of an effective police force or national militia allowed for continuous brutality, brawls and feuds. The ordinary citizen faced the unpredictable violence of armed knights. Those Iron Men, clad in their suits of armor often plundered whatever they wished, with little resistance from the vast majority of helpless people. Norbert preached peace and mercy and consideration to a world that was hardly a Camelot or the serene kingdom of an Ivanhoe.

In settlement after settlement he would find cases of armed combat and hatred. In addition he encountered a demoralized clergy, lonely, often practicing concubinage and feeling that the official Church cared little about them. He had plenty of work to do when hearing out the complaints of the serfs, who were little more than slaves caught in a hopeless situation of bondage.

At the same time Norbert came in touch with reforms. In Paris he would have witnessed the Canons of St. Victor—that is, parish clergy who adopted the ascetic ideals of William of Champagne. At Clairvaux and Citeaux he would have beheld the Cistercian reforms of the world of the monks. He noted that their churches had plain wooden crosses and walls bare of pictures or stained glass, that their diet was vegetarian and that they were allowed only six hours of sleep a night, while they were required to work at least seven hours a day in manual labor, mostly farm work. He also became acquainted with the Cistercian administrative system that created an international

federation of monasteries with a fair amount of
centralized power, though local houses had a certain
amount of independence. These reforms, written up in
their "Charter of Charity" would affect him
significantly in his own future work.

In the year 1120 he came to the city of Laon at the
request of Bishop Bartholomew, where part of his
assignment included the spiritual renewal of the
Canons of St. Martin's. Norbert failed to change them.
Bartholomew was convinced that Norbert had a great
deal more to offer and that he should stay in the area
and establish a community of priests very much in line
with his own personal ideals. After a considerable
number of conversations, Norbert agreed and
negotiations were begun to create a community of
canons regular.

Historian Barbara Tuchman notes in her study "A
Distant Mirror" that the Duke De Coucy, who was the
overlord of the area of Soissons, awarded a land grant
to Norbert in the valley of Premontre for the purpose of
establishing an abbey there. Norbert and a few
companions cleared out some of the land for a
settlement and rebuilt the ruined chapel of John the
Baptist.

On Christmas Day, 1120, Norbert and his friends
inaugurated the Canons Regular of Premontre, an
Order also called Premonstratensians—or more simply,
Norbertines. They swore to seek Christ by means of
community living, poverty, obedience, celibacy and a
dedication to the active priestly ministry. Norbert held
before them the dream of the first Christians after
Pentecost whose community life was characterized by
the power of the Spirit and a desire to be of service to
others.

For a Rule of life, Norbert chose the Rule of
Augustine as was common among communities of
clergy. In addition he adapted some of the customs of
the Cistercians. Even more of these would be brought

in later by Norbert's successor, Abbot Hugh of Fosse. It was his idea that his clergy would reflect the reforms for ministry instituted by Pope Gregory VII, and have the reformation spirit he had witnessed among the Cistercians. In effect he produced a community that would be somewhat monastic as far as house practice was concerned, and at the same time apostolic and evangelical when it came to active ministry. The whole idea was that his active priests needed an ascetic and contemplative haven, and that was the purpose of the abbey discipline.

In terms of numbers and growth his plan was hugely successful, for in a few generations there were Norbertine abbeys all over northern Europe. Within eight years, Norbert found himself nominated to be the Archbishop of Magdeburg. Like Augustine at Hippo, Norbert turned his residence into a Norbertine monastery and so carried to east Europe the ideals he instituted at Premontre. Always a man to be ready to develop his ideas further, he softened the monastic aspect of the lives of his men at Magdeburg, in order that they might have a more dynamic sense of outreach and commitment to active ministry. Experience had shown him that monastic practices tended to pull the men away from external ministry and to "withdraw" them too much from the world.

Even though Norbert was a man of deep prayer and spirituality, he was always a person agressively interested in the needs of the people. Almost certainly his many years as a missionary in France accounted for his action oriented mindset and therefore his ability to note the boundaries of inwardness that his abbeys observe. The administrative model of an international federation of abbeys did much to sustain these communities of canons and assure many of them centuries of survival as centers of service to the people and the parishes. Before Norbert's time, communities of canons tended to be individualized and isolated, lacking supervision, control and means of self renewal. The Norbertine canons surmounted this pitfall both by the above mentioned organizational model as well as by the unique adaptations Norbert made to the Rule of Augustine.

Norbert died in 1134, leaving behind him an example of ministry minded priests living in community—a model that was to become a norm about a century later.

Reflection

Norbert attempted to reproduce the lifestyle of the apostolic community of the early Church. In his theological outlook he saw the Holy Spirit as the originating power of the group. Common prayer and celebration of the Eucharist was to be the sustaining dynamic of the community. Selfless sharing and reaching out with love was the moral power that should surge from the members.

He dreamed of the emergence of a primary community whose members had the capacity to live together with a shared value system and shared beliefs. The first sentence of their Rule said, "Be of one mind and heart in God." Thus they were to have the ability to model and generate other communities based on divine love and human sharing.

By emphasizing the primacy of communal love in Premonstratensian existence, Norbert sparked all over Europe the possibilities for parish and other ministerial clergy to live in a soul satisfying community context. This is a goal still being sought for today.

Dominic

(1170–1221)

A Minister to Urban Culture

"Dominic, what book do you use to prepare your
sermons?" "I use only the Scriptures, the Book of
Love."

Dominic, A Class on Preaching

The economy of Europe from the Fall of the Roman
Empire until the dawn of the medieval period
(c. eleventh century) was primarily farming. Towns
served as little more than market centers and way
stations for travelers. Hence most of the Church's
Christianizing efforts concentrated on people involved
in an agrarian society.

However, towns and cities began to grow and take
on a special life of their own as commercial centers,
producers of consumer items and homes for the newly
prosperous urban types. Up to this point the rural
monasteries and abbeys served as points of vitality for
the Church. While many of the Norbertine Abbeys were
in Cathedral towns, most of them were still in the
countryside, and though their policy was outreach and
active ministry, their mindset basically reflected an
agrarian pastoral model.

What the Church needed as it moved into the twelfth
and thirteenth centuries was a pastoral model for
serving the developing urban centers. The solution was
found in the creation of the Mendicant Orders,
especially the Dominicans and Franciscans. City based

from the start, these Orders broke with the traditional financial method of sustaining monks and canons, namely, agriculture. More importantly, they replaced stability with mobility.

Rather than remain contained in fixed spots in tightly controlled areas, they chose to rove among the people from town to town and city to city, preaching the Gospel and showing them how to live as Christians in an urban setting.

In this chapter we will look at the pastoral method of Dominic and his followers, and discuss the Franciscans in the next one.

Spanish born, in Old Castille, Dominic came from a prosperous family who saw to it that he had a good education. He became a priest and joined the Cathedral Canons at Osma. Those clergymen followed the Rule of Augustine and had adopted many of the reforms of canons instituted by St. Norbert. Dominic soon became the Prior of the community and a close friend of the local bishop. He accompanied the bishop on several diplomatic trips to northern Europe and along the way encountered the heretical Cathari or "Puritan" communities in southern France.

It became apparent to Dominic, as it did to Church leaders everywhere that the Cathari posed a grave threat both to the true meaning of Christianity as well as to the stability of the social order, which was fragile enough anyhow. These Cathari-Puritans were a revival of the Manichean sect, to which Augustine had belonged. Because their central headquarters were at Albi, they were also called Albigensians.

Dominic correctly analyzed that the success of their appeal was their mastery of urban values and their self-awareness as a "new class" destined to replace the Feudal system. Dominic witnessed how they had developed an effective system of social services to the city poor, both as doctors and loan agents. He noted that they dominated the newly created weaving industries and made membership in their religion a requirement for becoming apprentices.

Dominic was quick to see how the Cathari acted as the commercial rulers, controlling the sales booths at fairs, markets and exchange offices. And when he saw that they used their homes as schools, making education of the young as yet another method for making converts, he realized that the Church was light-years behind in the new order that was emerging.

As a natural-born administrator and member of a ruling class, Dominic may well have grudgingly admired the skills of the Cathari. But as a Churchman he realized the enormous dangers inherent in their beliefs. They rejected Catholic sacraments and administrative procedure, and replaced them with their own rites and ruling processes. Their principal ritual was the *consolamentum,* a kind of general absolution from sins at the hour of death.

The Cathari elite were the so-called "Perfected," who pledged, "I promise to devote my life to God and the Gospel, never to have sex, never to kill an animal, never to eat meat and never to spend the night without a companion." The sexless elite often adopted children, and sometimes kidnapped them both to satisfy parental urges as well as to raise youth in their religion.

By refusing to recognize the legal binding force of any oath, they struck at the heart of the Feudal system based on loyalty oaths, thereby cutting the tie between urban dweller and rural overlord. Officially they were against paying taxes to princes, though in practice they often did. In a society where war was almost a norm, they professed pacifism—until the wars against them forced them to fight. They justified suicide for the terminally ill and for those who felt there was no other way to avoid temptations to sin. Suicide was either by means of self starvation or by mercy killing through suffocation by a member of the "Perfected."

Over a period of four lengthy journeys, Dominic had ample time to investigate the strengths and growing influence of the Cathari, whose presence was now confirmed in northern Italy and parts of central Europe. His contact with the demoralized clergy of southern France, the helplessness of the bishops, the widespread lay disaffection with the Church and the lack of leadership in the princes and lords who ruled the area, moved him to propose a new kind of moral mission and campaign to stem the Cathari tide.

With the approval of his bishop and the pope, he assembled a mission task force of educated and aggressive priests, whose personal lives were both beyond reproach and who were committed to the ideal of poverty. His group would "out-Puritan the Puritans," for while the Cathari lived in simplicity for the most part, they were personally prosperous. Dominic and his band of mobile preachers would be dedicated both to celibacy and poverty and thus demonstrate that these ideals could be lived in an urban setting and within the traditional teachings of the Church.

From 1206 onward, Dominic and his group debated with the Cathari leaders, preached authentic Christianity to the people at large and began to revitalize the presence of the Church. In the long run, Dominic's methods probably contributed the most to the successful reconversion of the area. This was not immediately apparent due to an unfortunate incident that provoked a violent war against the Cathari.

A sergeant of Count Raymond, the secular ruler of the area, assassinated the papal envoy. Pope Innocent III was angered both when Raymond did nothing to punish his sergeant and when he never supported any efforts to eliminate the Cathari. The Pope condemned the Count in an encyclical. The Bishops of France called for a crusade against the Cathari, thus unleashing a series of vicious civil wars that eventually had less to do with religion and much more to do with the usual outcomes of war—landgrabs, greed and power struggles. The whole affair was a battle between the Catholic North and the Cathari South. The Catholic forces won and installed their prince at Toulouse. The political and economic power of the Cathari waned and finally disappeared—as did their religion.

The upheavals caused by the wars did not distract Dominic from a concept of pastoral ministry that had an urban base and which he had tested successfully during the two years prior to the civil conflict, and continued to try out intermittently for the six years of the wars. His reflections led him to believe in the necessity of founding a new kind of religious order that would be in tune with the cultural values of towns and cities, namely, those of mobility, education and a democratic spirit.

Dominic resolved to take those values and wed them to certain traditional ideals of the monks and canons, especially the ascetical ideal of poverty, the prominence of prayer and the central calling to Christian love in community. His deliberations led him to create the Order of Preachers—the Dominican Order as it has been generally known. Dominic situated the central house at Toulouse, the very city where the new Catholic control of southern France had been established.

Dominic based the Rule of the Order on that of Augustine as already modified by Norbert. He decided that houses of the Order would not be permanent residences for the brothers (or "friars"), but that each member should be ready to go wherever needed. Preaching the Gospel was to be the chief duty of the brothers, but learning was presupposed. To make sure of this, Dominic insisted that every major Dominican house should be a house of study, with at least one resident professor. Manual labor was dropped in favor of study and active pastoral ministry.

The government of the Order would be collegial and democratic in style, involving the election of superiors and the resolution of Order questions and problems at regular meetings of the groups. Dominic was a planner, carefully supervising the constitutions and attending to all the details of basic policy.

He was responsible for founding numerous houses of his Order, to the point where eight provinces existed from Spain to Romania at the time of his death. He also began houses for the Dominican nuns, the first being at Prouille, a house designed to take in Cathari converts and assist them to become Christians and help them to start a new life in the world.

Throughout the centuries his friars have remained faithful to the active pastoral ministry he envisioned for them, and they broadened their calling to include the field of theology, so much so that by the end of the thirteenth century over seven hundred of them were engaged in teaching theology. It was out of this Dominican matrix that there emerged one of the greatest Christian theologians of history, Thomas Aquinas.

Reflection

Dominic's genius was to see, far in advance of many others, the new cultural direction the world was taking from rural to urban self-awareness. His eight years of evangelizing among the Cathari convinced him of the accuracy of his insight and the need to found an Order to respond to the new situation. He succeeded mightily, much to the benefit of Christianity and its goals. He read the "signs of his times" correctly. Vatican II asks us to do the same.

Francis of Assisi

(1182–1226)

A Brother to the Poor

"Lord, make me an instrument of your peace. Where
there is hatred, let me sow love. O Master grant that I
may never seek to be consoled as to console. . . ."
Prayer of St. Francis

The twelfth-century revival of commerce caused the
rise and expansion of towns and cities with a
concentration of new wealth. The shift of masses of
people from the farms to the towns posed a problem for
the Church whose pastoral models fitted the rural
based economy and culture. Dominic fashioned an
Order to minister to the prosperous, educated classes
who constituted the leadership in these new civic
centers.

The Church also needed a method for reaching the
masses of poor people who clustered in slums around
the walls of the old medieval cities and the new towns.
The answer was found in the person and vision of
Francis of Assisi.

The son of a prosperous cloth merchant, and very
much a city person, Francis was gifted with a sunny
personality, a voracious love of life and a poetic
temperament. He seems to have had an enormous
capacity for enjoying whatever he was doing, such as

the indulging in the latest fashions in men's clothes, long nights of partying, or just simply being with people. In very much this same spirit he identified with the prevailing romantic ideals of the shining knight, the noble warrior—chivalrous, courteous, and generous to the defeated.

It was in this spirit that he became a soldier in the perennial battles between Assisi and the neighboring Perugia. His brief career in the military, which included a period of defeat and imprisonment, disillusioned him. The viciousness of mortal combat, the curses, the naked hatred, the numbing humiliations of a jail brought him to a moment of truth and an experience of radical self-evaluation.

He felt within himself an irresistible call to follow Jesus Christ. When he saw the hordes of the new poor, packed in misery and hopelessness around the towns and cities, he resolved to take the message of Jesus literally, convinced that this was the best way to help these people. He, who had been daring and brave enough to engage in hand-to-hand combat, now discovered in himself the moral courage to let go of his wealth, security and family power base. In his mind he was completely persuaded that this was the way to follow Jesus and help the poor whose presence began to haunt his awareness. Still the chivalrous romantic, he switched from being the military knight doing brave deeds for the approval of the woman of his dreams to the spiritual knight wedded absolutely to "Lady Poverty."

The scene with his family, in which he repudiated his inheritance and tried to explain the reasons for his conversion, possesses all the elements of dramatic conflict that characterize the perennial misunderstandings between parents and young people. Anger. Harsh words. Love lamely expressed. Fixed positions. Irreconcilable attitudes. And apparently no happy ending, for biographers record no public reconciliation, though there may well have been forgiveness in the heart.

Francis then set out on his mission to bring hope to the poor and assist them toward a better future. Barefoot and penniless, he preached repentance and a simple message of trust in God and the exuberant enjoyment of God's goodness as felt and known in the wonders of nature. He showed rich and poor alike the sources of happiness in being free, in letting go, in permitting the beauty of the universe to flow into their souls. The affection and re-creative energy of "brother sun and sister moon" were the heritage of everyone regardless of the size of bank accounts.

The message of Francis proved appealing to ever growing crowds as well as to a circle of disciples who attached themselves to him. Gradually, these lay preachers—Franciscans—created an informal Rule of Life. As their numbers and influence grew, the suspicion arose that they might be another version of the disruptive "Poor Men of Lyons" who had been discredited about forty years before. Led by a devout layman, Peter Waldes, they also practiced and preached the merits of voluntary poverty. They were not "begging friars," like the followers of Francis, but they lived very simply, supporting themselves by work in the urban trades, like weaving.

They lived with the bare essentials, opposed the amassing of wealth, avoided taverns and dances and practiced celibacy. They had many of the traits of the early Puritans and Quakers. Trouble began when they took to the pulpits of churches to explain the Bible without any official permission. Moreover, they cited only the texts that dealt with poverty and hard work. Had they remained just single-minded enthusiasts for these values, they might have escaped opposition. But when they began attacking the lifestyles of the clergy and the bishops and alienating the people from the official Church, they incurred formal censure. Then they grew more extreme, claiming they alone were the real Christians, that the Pope was the source of error, the bishops were the new Scribes and the monks the descendants of the Pharisees, that the sacraments were useless and that the whole system for financing the Church was fundamentally evil. Predictably, they came under Papal ban and secular harassment and disappeared as a spiritual force in the Church.

With this memory fresh in many minds—and also the fact that pockets of this sect still existed in many parts of Europe—the Church leadership had reservations about Francis and the "Poor Brothers" of the Assisi-Perugia area. Francis went to Rome to defend his vision and the work of his brothers to Innocent III. He overcame the fears and suspicions of the Pope and received from him an oral approval to continue his work. Francis promised obedience to the Pope.

Very quickly after that the Friars experienced a remarkable expansion, preaching all over Italy, inspiring the people with their simplicity, informality and good cheer. They spoke in the vernacular everywhere, in the fields as well as town squares. They mastered the techniques of the spiritual revivalists and invented new popular devotions such as the Christmas Crib and the Stations of the Cross. Populist to the core, like Francis, they established a Christianity for the urban poor that was a mixture of penance and self-discipline—precisely the values needed, not only for gaining heaven, but also for obtaining upward mobility in the new socio-economic order that was developing. Thus the Quaker and Puritan instincts for a simplicity that led to prosperity were preserved, while the anti-clericalism and sectarianism were rejected.

In this light Francis is a social reformer consistent with the temper of the culture. By preaching and example he communicated a sense of self worth to the poor, awakened in them the planning instincts that would show them how to adapt to and take advantage of their new environment, and provide them with a spiritual ritual that satisfied their inner lives. His preaching of penance to a people already mortified by poverty, produced in them the disciplinary attitudes that made their capacity to survive and succeed a genuine possibility and offered them resources of inner hope which they sorely needed.

Of course he also witnessed poverty to the rich as well, with his "soft sell" and "laid back" posture. Although this approach lacked the thunder of Old Testament prophets, such as Jeremiah and Isaiah, it was more subtly effective. His strategy of being evocative rather than provocative worked its magic on many of his prosperous listeners, moving them to simpler lives and persuading them to create conditions for the improvement of the lives of the poor. He presented as graphic an example of evangelical poverty as one might ever wish to see.

Part of his success was due to the fact that he was so essentially a medieval romantic, almost shamelessly employing the imagery of romance and chivalry so appealing to the listeners. He knew their idiom and used it expansively. Yet underneath it all was the bone hard call to selfless love and the ideals of utter simplicity. It's not that he was deceiving his listeners, rather that he was capable of making the call in a language and personal witness that completely rang true to them.

Few saints of history have ever been so popular as Francis of Assisi. The Middle Ages loved him every bit as much as he loved his times. Writers and artists have surrounded his life with a vast network of legends and folklore, always identifying him with Christ and frequently referring to him as a New Adam in a medieval garden of Eden. The affectionate intent of these nostalgic reflections is sometimes undermined by its intensive sweetness. These images may entertain and charm us, but they tend to hide the man.

Francis was not above using the cultural conceits of his times, but he was personally anything but a soft, mellow man in the amber tones of a Giotto painting. For one thing he must have been a vulnerable man, absorbing a lot of pain in his life as he empathized with those suffering people he met. Because of his mystical bent, he united his pain with the Christ of the Passion to the point where he received the gift of the *stigmata*, the physical wounds of Christ in his hands, feet and side.

Another grief he bore, not always so sweetly, was the evolution of his Order into such a size that it required a formal Rule and some modification of the literal practice of poverty he wanted of them. Still, history has vindicated his basic poverty insight and his Order has been an authentic bearer of his spirit for over seven centuries. This is true as well for the Franciscan Sisters founded by Clare.

When Francis was about to die, he asked to be laid directly on the earth that he might have the closest possible touch with the creation through which he had always seen the presence of the Creator.

Reflection

G. K. Chesterton writes of Francis: "Before Dante, Francis had given poetry to Italy; before St. Louis ruled, he had risen as tribune of the poor; before Giotto painted, he enacted the scenes. . . . He was above all a great giver, and he cared chiefly for the best kind of giving which is called thanksgiving. This is the full and final spirit with which we should turn to Francis; in the spirit of thanks for what he has done."
(St. Francis of Assisi, pp. 230–1)

Catherine of Siena

(1347–1380)

She Changed the Mind of a Pope

"It seems to me that divine goodness is preparing to change furious wolves into lambs, and I will bring them humiliated to your bosom. Oh Father, peace, for the love of God."

Catherine, Conversation with Gregory XI

History is a record of the "best of times and the worst of times" as Dickens expressed it. Barbara Tuchman persuasively judges the "calamitous fourteenth century" to be among the worst of times, a period afflicted by the Black Plague, the Hundred Years War and the Avignon Papacy. The Plague killed well over a third of Europe's population. The War was an epic of brutality and bravery checkered by disgrace. The Papacy at Avignon was engulfed in a web of financial corruption to the point where its spiritual influence was nearly bankrupt.

This is the woeful world into which Catherine of Siena was born, the twenty-third child of her family. She proved to be a precocious child, strong willed and spiritually inclined. By the age of seven she already concluded she would not marry, but be "betrothed to Christ" and demanded—and received—her own room in the already overcrowded house. At the age of sixteen she became a member of the Third Order of St. Dominic. She followed the rules for nuns, while living as a layperson in the world.

Strongly drawn to meditation she eventually began to have mystical experiences, characterized by trances and raptures, especially after receiving Communion. Catherine wrote that Christ confirmed her betrothal to him through a series of spiritual communications. Like many medieval mystics, such as Bernard of Clairvaux, she was much taken with the biblical "Song of Songs." She read it constantly, often repeating the sigh of the bride, "May he kiss me with the kiss of his mouth." She testifies that Jesus did come and bestow on her "a kiss which filled her with unutterable sweetness."

She yearned to be fixed in perfect faith and become the instrument for the salvation of souls. She tells us that Jesus heard her prayer and took her for his bride in a ceremony performed by his Holy Mother and attended by St. John, St. Paul, and St. Dominic, with music from David's harp celebrating the event. Closely allied to her ecstatic experiences were acts of extreme deprivation of sleep and food and comfort.

The mystic Catherine was also an outgoing person, totally committed to caring for people in extreme need. She visited the prisons and volunteered long hours at the hospital and did what she could to relieve the problems of the poor. When the plague of 1374 struck Siena, Catherine was active in helping the victims who included ten members of her family. Blessed with abundant native common sense and a warmhearted sympathy, Catherine was frequently approached for advice. She dispensed her sensible opinions volubly and generously.

Since many of her mystic trances occurred in church after Communion, she naturally became the subject of much attention, conversation and curiosity in Siena. Her good works as a Dominican Tertiary would have won respect and appreciation for her, especially since she was known to deal with the most undesirable cases. But it was her mystical life that awakened the popular interest in her, a reaction that ranged all the way from skepticism, irreverence, hostility, incredulity to the more positive attitudes of belief and openness.

By the time she was twenty-three, she was surrounded by a group of spiritual-minded people, of all ages and walks of life, who looked to her as a guide for meditation, prayer and personal moral improvement. This utterly self-confident young woman accepted this responsibility as a spiritual leader, referring to her followers as "her family—her children." With no apparent embarrassment, they returned the compliment and called her *Mamma.*

Since she had no wealth, nor social standing, nor any other public source for her authority, she needed some official backing, an affirmation she received from the Dominican Order. The Dominican priest, Raymond of Capua, served as her Confessor as well as a kind of validator of her ministry by his constant presence. He supervised the "secretarial pool" that wrote out the enormous amount of dictation of which Catherine was capable. Raymond himself did some of the secretarial work, sometimes falling asleep in the wake of her voluminous outpouring.

In the first few years most of Catherine's energies focused on spiritual matters, but for the last eight years of her life she concentrated on public matters, especially the Crusades and the Avignon Papacy. An ardent *defender* of the Crusades, she was a strenuous *opposer* of the Avignon Papacy. It was her judgement—indeed God's will synonomous with her own—that the Pope belonged in Rome. She began writing letters to rulers, prelates and executive councils, freely dispensing to them both spiritual and political advice.

Her platform rarely wavered from the two issues of the Crusades and Avignon. To the King of France she writes, "Do God's will and mine." "I demand that you set forth and fight the infidels." Her idea was that Christians should have peace at home with each other, and that if they are going to fight, they should do so with the Turks.

Closest to her heart, however, was the issue of Avignon. The Papacy must return to Rome and extricate itself from the financial bondage and moral corruption of Avignon. The government of Florence, then at war with the Papacy, delegated Catherine to go to Avignon and help negotiate the possibility of peace with Gregory XI. Catherine gladly accepted and traveled to "Babylon on the Rhone" with the primary intent of convincing the Pope to move to Rome.

She stayed there for four months, depressed by what she called the "stench of sin" and the stupidity of the great ladies who ventured into the chapel after Communion to pinch her body and pierce her foot with a needle during her trances to test their validity. Raymond acted as her interpreter during her many conversations with Gregory, for she spoke Tuscan, and he, Latin.

With no hint of shyness, nor the slightest evidence of intimidation she used a forthright approach with the Pope. "Be a man Father! Arise! Don't be negligent!" Sometimes she called him, of all things, Sweetest Daddy, *dolce babbo mio.* In a thousand ways she stated her plan for the Pope. "Begin the reform of the Church through appointing worthy priests. Make peace in Italy, not by arms, but by pardon and mercy. Return to Rome, not with swords and soldiers, but with the Cross and the Blessed Lamb. O Father! Peace, for the love of God."

There probably have never been Papal audiences like these before or since. What Florentine and Roman diplomats had been unable to persuade, what the king of France had attempted to deter, Catherine achieved. Theologians tried to discredit Catherine and came out

of a twelve hour meeting, drawn, tired—and converted.
The totally self-assured Catherine sat easily in the
center of power, stared down the mighty and changed
the mind of a Pope. The "dolce babbo" agreed with his
mystic "mother," especially after she clairvoyantly
reminded him, "Who knows God's will so well as your
holiness, for have you not, when you were a Cardinal,
vowed that the Papacy should be returned to Rome?"
That probably shook him as much as anything, since
he had indeed made such a personal vow to himself,
should he ever become Pope. He had never told a
living soul. Now this young woman before him knew
his secret.

Up to the last minute the French King and the
Cardinals tried to stop Gregory. Charles V told him
"Rome is wherever the Pope happens to be." The
Cardinals arqued that if he went to Rome, there may
never be a way to end what was becoming a "hundred
years war" between France and England. As a
Frenchman, he hated the thought of leaving his
homeland. He worried about his health and grew
intensely nervous when he heard that a storm had
ruined some of the Papal ships. At the last moment, in
a scene worthy of a Verdi opera, the Pope's aged father
threw himself on the ground before his son and pleaded
with him to stay. Gregory stepped over the prone body
of his father and ungallantly recited this psalm verse,
"It is written that you shall trample on the serpent and
tread down the basilisk." Then as the bishops moaned,
"O God, if only the mountains would move and block
our way," Gregory XI sailed for Rome.

Meanwhile, Catherine took the overland route back
to Siena. Now she was an international celebrity,
mobbed by curious and admiring crowds in town after
town. In her own mind she had more important things
to do than to be coping with the burdens of fame. Her
experiences of the evils at Avignon released a flood of

reflections in her mind that required recording. She would be keeping her secretaries well occupied. Moreover, in her thirtieth year, her health was failing. She would have only three years to live.

Back in Siena she began dictating her Avignon Memoirs, those chapters of her "Dialogues" that deal with sinful priests as the bad servants of God. Comments such as these: "Their self love has made sensuality the ruler of their hearts. They are ignorant of the divine office. They behave like animals at the gambling houses, betting away their souls to the devil and gambling away property of the Church, so that the poor do not get what they need and deserve. This is the 'purity' the priests offer Me, that in the morning he rises with his soul defiled, having slept in his mortal evil, and in that state he stands before my altar."

Catherine of Siena died, in her thirty-third year, on the Sunday before Ascension. Her last words were full of self-reproach that she had not loved as deeply as she knew was possible. No one agreed with her. Their *Mamma* had loved more than any of them had believed possible.

The universal Church concurred canonizing her a saint in 1461, and making her a co-patron of Italy— along with Francis of Assisi—in 1939.

Reflection

One is tempted to judge, in transactional analysis terms, that Catherine adopted a parent-child relationship in her dealings with others thus avoiding the maturer and more desirable adult-adult ideals. That seems to be a superficial evaluation of an unusually gifted person, and based upon an anachronistic interpretation of her mother-child talk. Against all odds for a woman of her time and station, she rose to the center of international power and changed the course of history. She was not dealing with children, nor did they act that way. Pope Gregory permitted her endearing "dolce babbo" address, but he remained until the end the calculating, measured chief executive of the Church, requiring four months of convincing by Catherine before he conceded. She relied on her visions and prayers as well as her tough-minded capacity to stay in there and negotiate. She was assertive in the best sense of the word. Because of that, the Papacy and the Church are deeply in her debt.

Joan of Arc

(1412–1431)

She Proposed Impossible Dreams

Inquisitor: "Do you consider yourself to be in the state of grace?" Joan: "If I am not, may God put me there. If I am, may he keep me in it."

From the Trial of Joan of Arc

Two of the major scourges of the fourteenth century were the Avignon Papacy and the Hundred Years War. Both were brought to an end by women saints. Catherine of Siena persuaded the Pope to go back to Rome. Joan of Arc convinced the Dauphin to take the crown as lawful king of France as well as to set in motion the military impetus that would conclude a century of war.

Religion and patriotism played a central role in the careers of each woman. Catherine integrated her mystical visions with her stout patriotic love of Florence, Italy. Joan merged her mystical voices with a fervent patriotic devotion to Orleans, France. Catherine functioned as a literary polemicist and tough personal negotiator to accomplish her goal. Joan took to the battlefield as a moral commander to achieve her purpose. Each woman overcame what still seems an insurmountable dilemma, namely how to influence the worlds of diplomacy and politics with the values of faith. Their achievement would be extraordinary in any age. That they were able to do it all remains an inspiration for all believers who would affect the geopolitical order in any age.

Joan of Arc was born on the feast of the Epiphany in a France that was ruled for the most part by England, with the cooperation of the Duke of Burgundy. An English administrator served as a kind of colonial governor in Paris. The heir to the throne of France (the crown prince or "Dauphin") held some control over parts of southern France, but he lacked the aggressiveness even to go through with the ceremony of coronation after his father's death. A spiritless ruler, he communicated a defeatist attitude to his people and military commanders.

It seemed only a matter of time before France would be completely subdued and "pacified" so that it would be simply part of England, thus bringing an end to the Hundred Years War in this manner. It was the darkest moment of the country's history, as the people anticipated a future in which, as a colony of England, their money and talent would be used to make a foreign nation richer and more powerful.

The symbolism of Epiphany as a feast of light, Joan's birthdate, foretold the source from which France would find its salvation. When Joan was thirteen she began to hear the voices of St. Michael, St. Catherine and St. Margaret. Through them God commanded her, not to a life of religious fervor, but to undertake political action to rescue her country. Joan listened to their urgings for nearly three years before she was convinced she should go to the chief of staff of the French forces with her message.

Just as it took Catherine of Siena many months to wear down the resistance of Gregory XI, so Joan spent many tedious interviews attempting to persuade the French commander at Valcoeurs that her visions were genuine and her goal attainable. He had laughed at her, suggested he turn her over to his soldiers for sex, and ignored her for weeks. Still she came back until he capitulated. He brought her to the Dauphin at the castle of Chinon.

Joan entered the crowded audience room, where the Dauphin had decided to test her. He had disguised himself as a servant. Joan singled him out and approached him with these words, "Dauphin, I am Joan from Domremy. The King of heaven sends me to you with the message that you shall be anointed and crowned in the city of Rheims, and that you shall be the lieutenant of the King of heaven, who is the King of France." He took her aside and questioned her. During their conversation she, like a mind reader, told him of a prayer he had secretly made on the last All Saints Day.

He had prayed to know if he was the real king of France, for his mother had testified at the Treaty of Troyes that there was some doubt abaout his legitimacy. So he simply wasn't sure that the royal blood of his father ran in his veins. Joan argued that he was the real king and should be crowned as such. This unassertive, nervous man began to see the light. It was February 25, 1429.

Strongly in Joan's favor through all of this was her positive attitude. She was thinking the unthinkable, proposing impossible dreams, resolutely upbeat in a milieu of defeatism. She was soliciting springs of hope when the entire leadership had basically surrendered.

Their skepticism was not esily overcome. Mystic charlatans and "witches" were common enough in that period and they were never to be trusted. The Dauphin, Charles, decided on one more acid test. He sent her to be examined by a board of theologians at Potiers. There is no existing record of the proceedings, which is peculiar since such records are customarily preserved, and especially strange since the life of Joan of Arc is one of the best documented lives of a saint in history. What we do know is the verdict of the group. They recommended that the Dauphin follow her advice.

Six weeks after her meeting the Dauphin at Chinon, Joan's dream was about to come true. Joan was in control. An army was reassembled for the purpose of lifting the eight month siege of Orleans. On April 27th, Joan rode forth with the French army. Suited in armor and carrying a flag upon which was painted an image of the world upheld by two angels, and a portrait of Christ surrounded by the words *Jesus* and *Mary*, Joan was at last on her way. Contrary to popular myth, Joan never served as a military commander or strategist. She saw her role as a moral leader, as exemplified by her insistence that all the soldiers go to confession, and that all the prostitutes be left behind. Of course she also provided the inspiration and morale the troops would need.

When they came in sight of the city, Joan was taken by a safe custody detachment to a route that would enable her to enter the city. (The English surrounded it only on three sides.) On April 29th she rode into a jubilant city. At her insistence there should be no fighting until diplomatic missions calling for a truce or surrender failed. This went on for four days, on the third of which she appeared on the battlements and shouted to the English to make peace. They jeered her with the epithet, "Cowgirl."

On May 4th the fighting began, and Joan obtained her first taste of battle. She killed no one nor did she wish to do so. On May 8th the French troops inside Orleans and those which had come from Chinon made an all-out effort. Still unsuccessful after twelve hours of fighting, they decided to stop. For the first time Joan forced on them a military decision. They must keep on. They returned to battle with Joan in their midst. She was hit by an arrow. After her wound was treated and bandaged she returned once more to the struggle. Her presence gave the men that kind of mystic energy, that second wind, that moved them to do the impossible. They defeated the English and lifted the siege of Orleans.

All the resources of medieval pageantry broke loose, as all the bells of Orleans rang out and the people sang the Te Deum, thanking God, a whole list of French saints—and Joan of Arc, who from that day on would be known as the Maid of Orleans. The French had not won a great military victory, so much as a desperately needed psychological conquest of their own ineptitudes and defeatist mentalities. This was their turning point. They were on their way to ending the Hundred Years War.

And Joan was on her way to tragedy, betrayal and martyrdom within a year. This night they roared out her praises. Twelve months later, not one of them was willing to lift a hand to help her, not even the Dauphin whom she now led to Rheims to be crowned as Charles VII.

After the coronation, Joan noted that the king began to grow listless again. Moreover the military leaders, never at ease with Joan's presence among them and probably somewhat ashamed that it was she and not they who managed to re-inspire the fighting spirit of France, advised the king to pay less attention now to her advice. Joan refused to give up that easily and prevailed upon the king to capture Compegiegne, held at that time by the Burgundians who were in league with the English.

It was in that campaign that Joan was captured. The Burgundians sold her to the English to be tried as a witch and heretic before a Church court, chaired by the French Bishop Cauchon of Paris. As the record of the trial shows, it was not an exercise in justice but rather a prejudiced attempt by the English to discredit her credibility, especially her claim that she was moved by God. They could not tolerate such a claim, for that would mean that God was against the dominion of the English in France.

They started with intimidation, only to find Joan a sturdy witness. Asked to swear on the Gospels that she would answer nothing but the truth, she replied she did not know what they wanted to ask her. "Perhaps you may ask me things that I will not tell you." She shot this bold remark at a court composed of one cardinal, six bishops, thirty-two doctors of theology, sixteen bachelors of theology, seven doctors of medicine, and one hundred and three other associates.

They tried everything to break her, legal tricks of all kinds, hours and weeks of exhausting questions. She sat there alone, with no Charles VII or any French friend to help her. The court finally used torture to get a spurious confession from her. When she recovered from the torture and saw what they had forced her to sign, she repudiated it and attributed her "confession" to weakness. She never gave in again. The court found her guilty and sentenced her to be burned at the stake, May 30, 1431. She was nineteen years old.

Twenty-five years later, a papal court went over her case again and this time judged her to be innocent. The Church canonized her in 1920 and two years later declared her the patroness of France.

Reflection

Joan was like a meteor flaming brightly for three years and then literally burning out at the stake. Her short public life remains to fascinate us with its inspiring boldness and its paradoxes. Joan the woman who loathed killing, riding with and encouraging an army. Joan the peasant able to move easily with royalty and the military elite. Joan the person of "simple faith" confounding a legion of theologians. Joan the woman dressed in a man's armor. Joan the positive thinker in a defeatist world. Today's theologians are talking of a Jesus who frustrated conventional expectations to reveal the kingdom. That seems to be one of Joan of Arc's special gifts as well. In fighting for the kingdom of France, she did something even more worthwhile, she gave us a glimpse of the kingdom of God.

Thomas More

(1478–1535)

A Balanced and Principled Man

"God made the angels to show him splendor, as he
made the animals for innocence and the plants for
simplicity. But Man he made to serve him wittily, in
the tangle of his mind."

More, A Man For All Seasons

As a young lawyer, Thomas More belonged to what
was called the "Cenacle at Oxford," a group of
Christian Humanists that included John Colet and
Erasmus of Rotterdam. These bright young men were
dedicated to a reform of society and the Church by
means of education and proper role modeling, working
from the assumption that learning would increase piety
and that knowledge would improve people's moral
lives.

Rebellious in spirit, they repudiated the traditional
ways of studying philosophy and theology in the
Church. Colet summarized their position with his
comment, "It is sufficient to abide by the Bible and the
apostles, and let the theologians dispute among
themselves." Erasmus was relentless in directing his
Dutch wit and sarcasm, not only against clerical
abuses, but also some revered religious traditions.
More, in his *Utopia,* made sly sallies against religious
and political follies.

On the positive side, these Humanists emphasized
the historical nature of Christianity and stimulated the
study of the sources, especially the Bible and the
Fathers of the Church. They improved the study of

ancient languages and the methods of evaluating the texts. The best of these contributions came from the testy Erasmus in his splendid edition of the Greek New Testament and updated versions of the writings of the Fathers of the Church.

A common trait of these Humanists, aside from their radical positions, was an affection for the Old Church. Thomas More remained loyal to the Church to the point of martyrdom. Son of a lawyer and a judge, More attended Oxford and became a member of Parliament. He became a celebrated and witty intellectual and was known for his shrewd legal perceptions. His friendship with Henry VIII dates from the time that he served as a tutor when Henry was a young prince.

After a brief involvement with the Carthusian Order, More decided that he should marry, saying "It is better to be a chaste husband than an impure priest." His wife, Jane Colt, bore him four children. A month after her death, More married a widow, Alice Middleton, a woman whom Erasmus characterized as "aged, blunt and crude." Nonetheless More loved her and needed her to look after his four children and the crowded home at Chelsea which More had converted into a lively center for Humanist conversation and intellectual exchange.

More must have been a man of prodigious energies to be capable of attending to his law practice, overseeing the "stimulating chaos" at Chelsea, writing books, reserving quiet time for his prayers and weaving his way nimbly through the political labyrinth as an under-sheriff of London, a diplomat to France, a parliamentarian and finally Chancellor of England.

Clearly more devout than Erasmus and certainly more tactful than Colet, More possessed the skill of avoiding extremes in an extremist age. A towering intellectual, he seemed to feel perfectly at home with the earthy Alice Middleton, though some conflict caused him once to say ungallantly, "Alice is neither a pearl nor a girl." An absolute champion of reason, as demonstrated in his Utopian vision of a world governed by reason, More never wavered in his religious faith and resolved to die for his vision of Christian commitment. He felt perfectly free to criticize the Church that he loved, but he never thought of abandoning the Church whose love he cherished.

A man of extraordinary balance in a most unbalanced age, More handled the "future shock" of his time with a sense of humor and poise that was rare among his contemporaries. The medieval period, which witnessed the *Making of Christendom,* was coming to an end. The Renaissance and Reformation, that effected the *Unmaking of Christendom* was in full force, unleashing the winds of change and the roar of transition. More played his part in bringing about some of that change, even as he managed to remain his own man through it all.

Discovery and constant change dominated his lifetime. Columbus discovered America when Thomas More was fourteen. By the time More was thirty-five, old Europe was preparing to quarrel fatally about its religion—and to run away from those fights by seeking new horizons, fortune and fame in the Americas. The geographical expansion found an echo in the psychological expansion of More as he wrote his *Utopia.*

When he set his pen to write that book, the ineffectual fifth Lateran Council was ending and Luther was nailing his ninety-five theses on a church door. Facing a world that was falling apart, More dreamed about an ideal world. Instead of being grim about all the change, More was positively lighthearted in his scenario for a new world. Granted that he was too much the scholar not to be serious about his invention, he remains ever a playful observer of the human condition.

In other words many of his questions in *Utopia* should be seen as having a mock-serious quality to them. Why worry about having private property?

Would it not be better to live in common like the monks? Why not kill the king who wants a war instead of allowing thousands of people who do not want any war to die? Do you think animals are immortal? If not, why not? Would you not agree that the country would be in better shape if all lawyers were thrown out of it? Would not divorce be the simplest way to solve a host of uncomfortable problems, were it allowed? Is it not true that society would be a much nicer place if only it were ruled by common sense?

More permitted himself to think aloud these unthinkable thoughts not because he believed them, but in order to help himself find out why he did not believe them, as is perfectly evident from his other writings and his behavior. He possessed what we call today an "open mind," but not the openness that thinks everything new is true, rather an openness that is willing to listen to fresh thoughts and evaluate them in a reflective manner.

He had proved he was capable of friendliness to the new thinking, as was clear from his leading position as a Christian Humanist. At the same time he was not intellectually credulous, swallowing all new ideas without some kind of critical sense. He championed many of the new freedoms, but he was too much the sound lawyer to advocate the popular naive attacks on law and order. When his son-in-law, William Roper claimed he was prepared to break every law in England to get at the devil (meaning Henry VIII), More flashed back with anger, reminding Roper that England was tied securely from coast to coast with the ropes of law. Whoever decides to cut those ropes must be prepared to face the overwhelming chaos that would result.

Of all the events in the life of More nothing is more captivating than his battle of wills with Henry VIII. This most Catholic king, who had written a book in *defense* of the seven sacraments, and for it received the title of "Defender of the Faith" from the Pope, was prepared to *offend* the faith by getting a divorce from Catherine, his Spanish-born wife. Depressed by the fact that she had not borne him a surviving male heir for the throne, fearful that the crown might pass to the Scottish kings, and convinced that a war of succession would be the result, Henry resolved to find a way to dissolve his marriage.

He appointed his chancellor, Cardinal Wolsey, to seek an annulment from the Pope, arguing that since he had married his brother's widow, he had entered into an invalid marriage. The Pope did not agree. Wolsey died, and More succeeded him, but not too enthusiastically, since he did not believe in the divorce and was not prepared to seek it or support it. The one time tutor of a young prince now faced a formidable King. He had given life to the mind of a boy. The King could take away the life of More's body—but proved powerless when trying to alter More's conscience.

When the King decided to break with the Pope and make himself the Head of the Church of England, More resigned the chancellorship, retired to Chelsea and resolved to preserve an absolute silence as to his opinion about the divorce and remarriage of the King to Anne Boleyn. More refused to take the Oath of Supremacy, acknowledging Henry as Head of the Church, and was silent about his reasons for this.

Totally familiar with law and with the ways of kings and the intrigues of the court, he realized he was in extreme peril for his life and was virtually destroying the financial base and future of his family. They knew it too and were not very pleased with him. What still remains as one of the most arresting features of the story is the fact that virtually every leader in England, layperson and cleric alike (with very few exceptions), took the oath. What was there about More the layman, ready as any Humanist to jibe at the folly of bishops, but fundamentally an "Old Church" loyalist, that he would stand up for the universal Church even when all the bishops and theologians went the other way? What was it that made him oppose Henry? Probably many things. Certainly among the reasons is the fact that More was a man of integrity and moral principle.

He was not given to dramatic defiance, nor did he ever poor mouth the King or reveal confidences. He did not court martyrdom, hoping in fact that his discretion, silence, and retired way of life might spare him. But More's very fame was against him. All Europe, all England, and the King knew that his silence was a daily moral judgement on the King. Seldom has silence been so effective a prophetic instrument. In the end, Henry could not endure life without More's approval, so he ordered imprisonment and a judicial murder. More is said to have retained his patience and good humor to the end, advising the executioner not to touch his beard which had done no harm. And then on a more serious note said, "Be not afraid, for you send me to God."

Reflection

An attempt to single out the most impressive aspect of More, the essential Renaissance man, witty, bright, devout, and engaged in a bewildering range of interests, is virtually impossible. Each time one approaches the life of Thomas More there is another compelling side of his person provoking attention and reflection. Our Anglo-Saxon culture, probably the world's most litigious, may find the lawyer in More the key to his personhood, especially since the final drama of his life revolved around the taking of an oath. Fair enough, for this is one access to his moral and spiritual attractiveness. Whatever one finds in More, it is bound to warm a faltering and cooled-off faith. How else is one to react to a man "who went so blithely to God"?

John Fisher

(1469–1535)

The Only Bishop To Say No

"Do you know, Robert, they are asking the only
working bishop in England to retire?"
John Fisher, Letter to His Brother

On the matter of his divorce, Henry VIII managed to
intimidate all the bishops of England into agreeing
with him, except one, John Fisher. Why did the other
bishops cave in with such apparent ease? One reason
is, they remembered this was not the first time that the
Crown and the Papacy had battled one another and
became friends again. Many of them felt that this was
a temporary break that was bound to be healed as
always before. So why lose one's life or base of
financial support over a passing dispute? After all, the
King was still upholding all the Catholic doctrines,
defending the Sacraments (save for matrimony) and
making no changes in the liturgy. And Wolsey had
been handling the Church court cases that used to be
sent to Rome, but no longer so. The Pope seemed far
away and their comfortable lives lulled their moral
sensitivities.

Why then was Fisher the lone exception? For one
thing he was a member of the community of Christian
Humanists, along with More, Colet and Erasmus,
whose loyalties remained with the Old Church, even
though they were aggressive reformers of it. Secondly
as an intellectual and theologian, Fisher possessed a
more sophisticated appreciation of the perils of Schism.

Lastly, fortified by a lifelong bent for asceticism, Fisher grew into a man of integrity and consummate moral principle, who knew how to say no when his conscience demanded it.

Born of a Yorkshire merchant, Fisher studied theology at Cambridge University where he was ordained to the priesthood. Early on he demonstrated a love for scholarship in tune with the new humanism as well as a taste for administration. His career at Cambridge led quickly to a proctorship at Michaelhouse, a presidency at Queens College and ultimately the chancellorship, a post he held all his life—a unique distinction, since a life-time Chancellorship of Cambridge has been granted to no one else.

Fisher came to the attention of Margaret Beaufort, mother of Henry VII. She retained him as a confessor and a consultant in the disposition of her wealth. At Fisher's urging, she supplied the funds for building Christ's College and St. John's College at Cambridge, as well as financing a chair of theology at both Cambridge and Oxford. These "Lady Margaret Chairs" of theology exist to this day as the two most prestigious theological appointments in the Church of England.

Fisher fostered the flourishing of Humanist Studies at Cambridge, inviting Erasmus himself to come there and teach Greek. After Erasmus published his breakthrough critical Greek edition of the New Testament, Fisher decided to learn Greek himself and took his first lessons from the Dutch scholar. Erasmus was fond of Fisher and wrote of him, "He is the one man at this time, who is incomparable for uprightness of life, for learning, and for greatness of soul."

Along with his duties at Cambridge, Fisher was appointed the Bishop of Rochester. Situated between London and Canterbury, it was the smallest diocese in England, but it entitled Fisher access to centers of power and influence. Probably the smallness of his diocese made it possible to manage both a university and his episcopal see. He enjoyed being out among people and is cited as being an attentive, pastoral-minded bishop, visiting the parishes and promoting services for the poor.

Outwardly, Fisher appeared to be an ordinary Prelate, fond of entertaining friends, though clearly a lot more involved with his diocese than most bishops, and certainly more intellectual than his peers. One might estimate him as a good and bright bishop. At the same time, the private John Fisher, as in the case of so many of the saints, was an ascetic practicing the classic deprivations of sleep, food, comfort and discipline of his passions.

During his days as Bishop he was drawn into the controversies surrounding the teachings of Martin Luther. The matter was occasioned by Luther's attack on Henry VIII's work "In Defense of the Seven Sacraments." Luther employed his customary earthy and colorful style to assault the English monarch. "The King's book has been put forth to his everlasting disgrace. He was a fool for allowing his name to be abused by a parcel of empty headed sophists, reminding the world of such fat pigs as are mewed in the sty of St. Thomas. I have thought it right to snub and pinch him with sharp words. . . ."

Henry was of no mind to write a personal reply to Luther and may have agreed with his jester who said, "O good Harry, let you and me defend each other, and let the faith defend itself." In any case, Henry concluded that someone should rise to the occasion. One of those who did was Fisher, who proceeded to write eight books against heresy in general, including direct replies to Luther.

When Luther wrote, "Who will bring the Pope to order? Christ only, with the brightness of his coming. Lord, who has believed our hearing?" Fisher answers,

"There is no reason to believe your hearing, since you have heard what you say only from the devil. It is he who has whispered in your ears that the Pope is Anti-Christ. I am not unwilling to say that the Pope and his court should be reformed, if there is anything in their life divergent from the teaching of Christ. If it is necessary, would that they reform themselves."

The King was pleased with Fisher's defense in this matter. Twelve years later Fisher was called upon to defend the King's wish to annul his marriage with Catherine, and this time the King was not so satisfied with the Bishop of Rochester. Fisher reviewed the following elements in the case. Henry, being the second son of his father, was not the crown prince and heir to the throne. That was the right of his older brother Arthur, the Prince of Wales. Young Arthur was wedded to Catherine of Aragon in an arranged marriage between the Royal Houses of England and Spain. Arthur died soon after and allegedly never consummated the marriage.

The crown passed to Henry who decided to marry Catherine, his brother's widow. But there was a biblical impediment to the marriage as expressed in Leviticus 20:21. "The man who takes to wife the wife of his brother commits impurity." Henry sought a dispensation from the Pope. The Council of Constance had assured an earlier Pope that this matter was not so serious an injunction that a Pope could not dispense from it. Even though Popes could dispense, they rarely had. Julius II decided to grant Henry the dispensation he asked, so he could marry Catherine. It was only the second time a Pope had done so.

Now Henry was arguing that his marriage to Catherine was actually invalid, since taking a second look it was clear to him the Pope could not dispense from what the Bible said. Fisher examined the history of the case and concluded that the dispensation was correct and therefore the marriage of Henry and Catherine was a true and valid union. A legitimate dispensation of this kind could not be overturned.

When he wrote up his opinion on the case, Fisher quoted from Henry's own defense of the Sacrament of Matrimony and added his own comments. Fisher quoted, "Whom God has joined together, let no man put asunder. What an admirable expression! Who would not be pleased to know that God thought so much of marriage that He not only is present at it, but presides in it?" Fisher's comment, "The King's wife is Catherine. In his own words he is bound not only to love her, but live with her in a manner pleasing to God."

At the first formal hearing of the case, the Archbishop of Canterbury presented a list of the signatures of all the bishops of England favoring Henry's cause. John Fisher snapped, "That is not my hand or my seal." Canterbury nervously admitted it was a forgery in a sense, but that it was included since it represented Fisher's thinking. Fisher left no one in doubt, "There is nothing more untrue, my lord." Henry noted the lone dissenter and remarked that a single negative vote meant little when all the other bishops agreed.

The sixty-five-year-old Fisher committed himself to a position that would lead to his martyrdom a year later. The government harassed Fisher and tried to discredit him by implicating him in the case of "The Holy Maid of Kent," a Benedictine nun named Elizabeth Barton. Given to visions and trances, which at first dealt with matters of spiritual renewal, Sister Barton drew royal displeasure when she began to comment on Henry's immoral union with Anne Boleyn, noting the divine punishments that would afflict him for this. Fisher was accused of promoting her treasonous statements. His truthful reply was that he visited the nun to assess the validity of her claim that what she said came from God, and not for the purpose of approving or encouraging her political statements.

Nonetheless, Fisher was fined by the crown for his presumed crime. Six months later Parliament enacted laws making Henry the Head of the Church, the bishops subject to the Crown and the heirs of his marriage to Anne, legitimate successors to the throne. The bishops were required to sign an oath of agreement to this new state of affairs. Fisher refused, as did his friend, Thomas More. (Personally, More and Fisher agreed that Parliament could make the children of Henry and Anne heirs to the throne—though illegitimately born.) They were both committed to the Tower on April 17, 1534, where each man was kept under pressure to change his mind and submit.

Fisher followed More's example of silence on the matter, hoping thereby to protect his life without compromising his conscience. Richard Rich, the Attorney General for Wales, went to Fisher and asked him as a priest to give his opinion on the oath, for the King needed to know this as a matter of conscience. Fisher felt he could not refuse to speak when it was a matter of moral and spiritual guidance. He spoke his own death sentence, "The king was not, nor could ever be, by the law of God, supreme head of the Church."

Three weeks later, Henry ordered John Fisher's execution.

They buried him in the Tower Church of St. Peter in Chains.

The Church canonized him May 19, 1935.

Reflection

John Fisher presents convincing evidence that one can be a pastoral-minded bishop as well as a university intellectual, a skilled "brick and mortar" administrator along with being a man of exceptional moral courage, and a private ascetic who exhibits a genial and easy-going way of making others feel at home. There is a Dickensian cosiness about Fisher that attracts us even as it masks the moral toughness that solicits our attention the last year of his life. John Fisher may affect us by his principled strength.

Teresa of Avila

(1515–1582)

The Earthy Mystic

"A prioress may be very holy, yet incapable of
governing a community. In that case, she should
simply be removed from office."

Teresa, Advice to Visitators

The nuns were shocked and angry. The provincial of
their Order had just forced a new prioress on them.
Bad enough they were not permitted a voice for whom
they wanted, worse yet they were compelled to accept
a fifty-six-year-old nun, famous for being a reformer of
their Order according to the Rules for strict
Observance. One account reports that the 130 nuns
rose from their choir stalls, shouting and weeping and
protesting the violation of their voting rights.

The person they were protesting was Teresa of Avila,
who was herself personally against taking the job, and
assuming it only because ordered to do so under
obedience. The provincial remained firm and Teresa
became prioress of the Convent of the Incarnation.

When the Carmelite nuns assembled the next
morning to hear Teresa's opening remarks, they looked
in disbelief at the chair of the prioress upon which
stood a statue of the Virgin Mary, with the keys of the
convent in her hands. Teresa sat on an adjoining chair
and delivered an address that was a masterpiece of
tact and Christian affection.

"My sisters, this election has distressed me, for it
has deprived you of your freedom of choice and given

you a prioress against your will, a prioress who would be accomplishing a great deal if she could succeed in learning from each of you here all the good that is in you.

I come solely to serve you and please you in every possible way that I can. See then, my friends, what I can do for each of you. Have no misgivings as to how I shall govern you, for though I have lived among and governed nuns who are Discalced (of the Strict Observance), I know well enough the way to govern those who are not. I hope the Lord will greatly assist me to do this."

Over the next three years of her tenure, Teresa won their confidence, respect, and love as she succeeded in restoring the financial and spiritual matters of the convent.

Teresa was no stranger to this convent, for she had entered it thirty-five years before, and remained a member of it for twenty-seven years, at which time she began the convents of the Reform. When she entered the convent of the Incarnation of Avila, the young Teresa found a congenial and easygoing community of women, good spirited but not consumed with a spiritual fervor one might expect in a cloister.

If anything, the convent of the Incarnation was more like a genteel hotel for the unmarried, upper-class women of Avila. They did not observe the rules for cloister. They entertained guests in their rooms, treated the visiting area as though it were a hotel lobby, and some of them were given to wearing rings, bracelets and necklaces. They thought nothing of leaving the convent to spend weekends and vacations with friends and relatives. The sisters recited only the required prayers and otherwise distracted themselves with visiting and keeping up on the news.

Being very personable and an extrovert, Teresa enjoyed life at the convent of the Incarnation and fell right in with the cheerful and casual ways of the community. She liked to laugh, to sing, to dance and to talk, so her gregarious spirit found a circle of like-minded women at the convent. She differed from them only in her mounting suspicion and doubt that this was not what convent life should be all about.

After several years, her health began to fail. "The change in the habits of my life and in my food proved harmful to my health. I began to have frequent fainting fits and my heart was so seriously affected that everyone around me grew alarmed." Doctors seemed unable to help her, so she was taken to a famed woman healer in Becedas, whose use of violent purgatives nearly killed Teresa. Subsequently afflicted by paralysis of her legs and a damaged constitution, Teresa returned to the convent of the Incarnation where she remained in that state for nearly three years. She refused any further medical treatment, adopted a positive attitude toward her health and relied on prayer for a cure. By the end of three years her health returned and her paralysis disappeared.

While it is true that Teresa enjoyed and participated in the relaxed ways of the nuns of the Incarnation, she always felt an attraction to prayer and penance and did them with regularity. A major difficulty she faced was that an intellectual or imaginative method of meditation was advocated. One was either to imagine a scene from the life of Christ and dwell on that, or think about a concept of Christian doctrine and keep it one's awareness for awhile.

Teresa felt no attraction to either of these techniques and could not find a spiritual director who seemed to know what she needed. What she required was someone to tell her that she could meditate without benefit of ideas or imaginative representations. After nearly twenty years of struggling with this meditation dilemma, she discovered the solution for herself. One day, while meditating in the chapel she noticed a painting of Christ scourged at the pillar that had been newly placed there. The image stirred her deeply with compassionate empathy and she found herself moved into a deep tranquility, a nonconceptual, nonimaginative state of consciousness. She had stumbled onto what she was to call in her own writings, "The Prayer of Quiet."

Ironically, only after this personal discovery does she begin to meet spiritual guides, such as Francis Borgia and Peter Alcantara, who know what she is talking about and who could have pointed her in this direction in the first place. Perhaps it is just as well she learned it on her own, because that may account for her ability to write a scientific description of the multiple processes of prayer from meditation to what she called the "mystical marriage," a comparatively fixed state of conscious union with God.

Over the next decade Teresa began to soar inwardly in her experience of God. Her meditations were sometimes accompanied by raptures, ecstasies and trances. She was advised to write an autobiography and also an account of her spiritual experiences. Both of these books have become classics of spiritual literature, especially the "Interior Castle."

At the age of forty-eight she began a second career as the foundress of a reformed order of Carmelites, the Discalced nuns who wore peasant roped sandals instead of shoes. She found four women willing to join her in this new convent. She begged money from family and friends for a simple house to suit their needs, obtained the Pope's permission, and on August 24, 1562 moved with her novices into the new Carmel of St. Joseph.

Her rule was cheerful, loving and firm. The sisters slept on straw, ate no meat and stayed home. No visitors were allowed. The tiled floor served as beds, tables and chairs. She forbade begging, but did put a revolving disk in the wall upon which people could leave food if they wished. They eked out a small living by spinning and needlework, putting their products on the disk for the taking, leaving the buyer to put whatever he wished in return. This austere cloister began attracting new members. The provincial of the Carmelites was so impressed with St. Joseph's that he asked Teresa to start another Carmel in Medina Del Campo.

While working on the details of the new Carmel at Medina, Teresa was approached by the prior of the male Carmelite monastery who was interested in ideas for reforming his own lax friars. He was accompanied by a short, frail young Carmelite. Teresa remarked afterwards, "Bless the Lord, for I have a friar and a half for my new monastery." The little man was John Alvarez, destined to be the famed John of the Cross, the crown and glory of the Discalced Carmelite Friars.

Over the next eighteen years, Teresa was to establish sixteen more convents, amid a series of frustrations and anxieties that would have driven a lesser woman quite mad, or at least close to despair. Some of her difficulties came from the zoning boards of city councils who feared that her convents, not having the normal sources of funding, would become local welfare cases.

The strongest opposition came from the top administrators of the male Carmelites who followed the mitigated Rule. One report has it they went so far as to smuggle in an agent who pretended to be seeking affiliation as a discalced nun, but who afterwards falsely testified that Teresa flogged her nuns and heard confessions as though she were a priest. Teresa was summoned before the Inquisition which rendered this verdict, "You are acquitted of all charges. Go and continue your work." Hardly had she won that battle than she was faced with the opposition of the papal nuncio. She wrote for protection to King Phillip II who had read and loved her writings. The King summoned her for an audience, was convinced of her saintliness and granted her royal immunity. The papal nuncio changed his mind.

When not fighting political battles with these various opponents, Teresa was busy institutionalizing her eighteen convents and peppering them with her hard won wisdom, collected now as Teresa's "Maxims."

—Never be obstinate, especially in unimportant matters.

—Be kind to others, but severe on yourself.

—Habitually make many acts of love, for they set the soul on fire and make it gentle.

Perhaps the best insight into the practical nature of Teresa can be found in the many volumes of her published letters. There one finds the Teresa who argues with zoning boards, settles wills, negotiates purchases and offers down-home advice, as in the case of the Cistercian nun who was collapsing into lengthy trances for no apparent reason. Teresa looked into the matter, as one given to extensive trances herself, and found out the woman was suffering from malnutrition due to ill-advised fasting. "Feed the lady and she'll get better." And she did, never again to have a trance.

Teresa died, worn out and happy, at sixty-eight on October 4, 1582.

The Spanish government proclaimed her patroness of Spain in 1617.

The Vatican canonized her in 1622.

Reflection

In these days of nonconceptual forms of meditation, Teresa's theories of meditation should acquire a new pertinence. However, two major differences set Teresa's vision of meditation apart from the contemporary views. Teresa would quiet the mind and the imagination, opening the person's inner awareness to the influence of God. Secondly, this was done with the purpose of deepening the person's capacity to love God and people more intensely. Today's meditation schools concentrate mainly on relaxing the tension-ridden modern person, normally with no intention of being touched by God or seeking altruistic behavior. Some Christians are beginning to combine today's meditative techniques and Teresa' purposes. That practical-minded woman, Teresa, would not mind at all. She might well say, "Why didn't someone tell me that when I entered the convent of the Incarnation?"

Ignatius of Loyola

(1491–1556)

A Warrior for God

"As to fasts and abstinences, I would advise you to be careful. Strengthen your stomach for the Lord, and your other physical powers, rather than weaken them."
Ignatius, Letter to Francis Borgia

Born in the castle of Loyola, Ignatius was one of thirteen children. Raised to be a soldier, receiving little schooling, he displayed no interest in religion. An eager reader of romantic stories about courageous knights, he chose the wife of King Ferdinand as his "Queen of Hearts" at the time of his investiture as a knight. He wore her colors and dreamed of winning a lace handkerchief from her as a tournament prize. His secret love for her did not stop him from the occasional love affairs and brawls that characterized a soldier's life.

Ignatius spent four years of active duty in Pamplona until his leg was shattered by a cannonball during a battle with the French. The field surgeons set his bones and sent him home. Unfortunately, the bones were wrongly set, so they had to be re-broken and reset. The second operation proved to be more incompetent than the first for now a stump of bone stuck out, so he had to endure a third operation at which time the leg was finally straightened, but left a little shorter than his other leg. He spent frustrating weeks of pain as a stretching device secured his injured leg.

As the boring months of convalescence wore on, Ignatius asked for some books on chivalry to distract him, but the only books in the library were a life of Christ and a collection of lives of the saints. At the start, his militant tastes did not take to these apparently irrelevant stories. As time wore on the figures of Christ and Mary began to affect him. The lives of the saints proved to be as dramatic as the tales of courageous knights. In his mind he visualized the biggest war of all, that of Christianity against Islam. He would become a spiritual soldier, go to Jerusalem and liberate Christianity from the Moslems. He resolved to be a soldier of Jesus and Mary until his death.

Tradition held that the Holy Grail was hidden in a castle at Montserrat and that the knights of old would pray before the shrine of the Virgin there before undertaking their exploits. Ignatius decided to go there as a pilgrim and make that the departing point for his spiritual knighthood. Arriving at the Benedictine monastery of Montserrat, Ignatius gave away his fine clothes, donned a beggar's robe and spent a night before the altar of the Mother of God, pledging to her a vow of poverty and chastity.

After a few more days of prayer, he felt ready to go to Jerusalem and fulfill his dream. On his way he stopped at the village of Manresa and stayed the night in a cave. That evening a new awareness dawned on him that he had not begun to match or surpass the saints in their ascetical preparation for ministry. He canceled his immediate plans for Jerusalem and embarked on a year long, brutal bout of self-deprivations. Determined to crush his male vanity, he stopped washing, cutting or combing his hair. He wouldn't cut his nails or wash himself at all. He gave up meat, begged what little food he ate, scourged himself, slept little and prayed for long hours.

He almost killed himself and might have died, but for the fact that a sympathetic woman insisted on taking him home and nursing him back to health. She prevailed on him to move to the Dominican monastery where the watchful community might curb his extremism. He felt he still had not crushed the inner demons that tormented him, so he resumed his self scourgings and began to entertain thoughts of suicide. In this darkest hour the turnaround began. Visions of Christ, Mary and the Trinity surfaced in his awareness and strengthened and comforted him. Inner peace replaced his anxieties and a sense of hope drove out the despair with which he had wrestled during that long year of trial at Manresa. A genuine mystic, virtually intoxicated with God's presence, Ignatius captured the meaning of his soul battle in the epic-making document of religious guidance, *The Spiritual Exercises.*

Feeling thoroughly prepared, he traveled to Jerusalem only to face disillusionment. The Moslems allowed Christians to visit as pilgrims, but forbade any conversion efforts. The Franciscan provincial, mandated to keep peace in the Holy City, advised the dispirited Ignatius to go home.

Having brought his body under control, Ignatius decided to improve his mind. This thirty-three-year-old war veteran and newly honed mystic began a ten-year-long series of studies at Alcala, Salamanca and Paris. He also had the itch to teach and this caused him no end of troubles. In one place he gathered a group of religious-minded women around him for seminars on asceticism. The women's lovers were not at all pleased, so they thrashed him and threatened him with more if he did not stop.

He moved on and this time worked with poor women and prostitutes. A few of them started having trances, thus alerting the Inquisition to the activity of Ignatius. They tried him and put him in jail for two months until he convinced them he was completely orthodox. They released him but forbade him to teach. At Salamanca, Ignatius went through the same cycle of teaching, Inquisition, imprisonment and acquittal. That was enough for him. He saw no future in Spain, so he departed for Paris.

While Ignatius was completing his work on a master's degree in Paris, he attracted a group of men who would become the nucleus of his new religious order, the Company of Jesus, or Jesuits, as they would eventually be called. Chief among his new friends were Pierre Favre and Francis Xavier, the latter man coming from Pamplona where Ignatius had served as a soldier.

Ignatius put them through the paces of his Spiritual Exercises, a methodical, systematic route to prayer, and yet a flexible design for use in the distracting, noisy, complicated and man-made rhythms of the great cities of the world where the Jesuits were destined to minister. The express purpose of Ignatius was to bring his men to experience a spiritual conversion through a carefully planned series of meditations.

They were to begin with self-analysis, examining their selfishness, lust, avarice and other forms of human sinfulness, an exercise created to awaken in them the need for personal change. Next Ignatius brought them to realize that commitment makes the difference, for if they allowed the kingdom of Satan to command their allegiance then there will be no possibility of conversion, but if they surrendered themselves to Christ, then they have moved into the condition for conversion.

If they were willing to make their commitment to Christ, they must subsequently spend time meditating on the events of Christ's life, especially the saving Passion and Death of the Lord. Ignatius generally insisted on a vivid and personal identification of the meditator with the scenes from the Passion. This process was meant to assist the "exerciser" to realize that salvation is a gift of love that one must be freely willing to accept. The final phase of the Exercises led the person to contemplate the mystery of Easter and its effect on his continuing life as a Christian.

By these exercises Ignatius prompted his followers to remove themselves from the distractions of the city and to acquire an inner awareness of God's presence by means of fixing attention on some biblical scene or spiritual truth. He explained that they would have positive reactions of spiritual joy and that such consoling feelings would draw them towards Christ. At the same time they would also experience negative feelings of sadness and emptiness, the purpose of which was to reach a maturity to be able to seek the God of consolations, rather than the consolations of God.

If conversion and commitment occurred, then the seekers would begin to appreciate what is God's will for them. This would come about by uniting one's own thinking and faith yearnings with a quiet inner attention to signals that come from "resting in the Lord." Thus knowing God's will would be neither a mechanical, non-thinking yes to God, nor an act of logic that required no prayerful listening to the impulse of the Spirit.

The basic conversion that would result from the first round with the exercises was meant to be followed by a lifelong series of mini-conversions, in which the exercises would be returned to as part of one's "growth plan."

After Ignatius and his small group of followers had completed the exercises, they went to a chapel in Montmartre and took vows of chastity and poverty. They further pledged themselves to go and live in the Holy Land after two more years of study. Circumstances frustrated their Palestine plan, so they went to Rome instead and put themselves at the service of the

Pope. They were formally approved as a religious order by Paul III in his papal bull *Regimini Militantis Ecclesiae* (For the Rule of the Church Militant).

The men elected Ignatius as their first General. He set about immediately writing a Constitution for the Order. For the next sixteen years he presided over an astonishing expansion of growth in membership and influence. By the time of his death, a thousand Jesuits ministered as educators in one hundred colleges, as missionaries in China, Japan, India and major parts of North and South America. They mingled actively in the affairs of the world as prudent and tactful men, following the maxim of Ignatius that more prudence and less piety were better than more piety and less prudence. Ignatius sternly stressed discipline and obedience, but never to the point of breaking the man's will or destroying his initiative. As a former soldier he realized that willingness to obey is the first step in learning to command, and his insight proved correct, for the Jesuits were clearly a group of enterprising men who took easily to leadership positions.

Ignatius died on July 31, 1556, having achieved his three goals for the Jesuits: (1) the reform of the Church through education and frequent participation in the sacraments, (2) a vital missionary thrust and (3) an aggressive stance toward heresy. The Church canonized him in 1622.

Reflection

Ignatius founded the most successful educational order in modern history, yet personally put little stress on learning or intellect. His order was to produce legions of theologians, but he himself preferred direct perception of God, convinced as he was by an overpowering awareness of God, Christ, Mary and the saints. His mystical bent did not prevent him from being a genius of an organizer. He knew how to be tough and flexible at the same time. He judged people shrewdly and became one of the most influential men of modern history. The rugged, romantic soldier of Pamplona became a God-intoxicated religious leader. Few men have made such a transition so well. Few have ever done so much, as Ignatius liked to say on his own behalf, "For the greater honor and glory of God."

Phillip Neri

(1515–1595)

God's Clown Converts Rome's Elite

"I am considering the greatness of God. The more I consider it, the more it seems to grow before me, and its very immensity forces me to step backwards."

Phillip Neri, Dialogue with Tarugi

Phillip Neri worried a lot about his image. He was determined people would not mistake him for a saint, so he adopted eccentricities designed to make people think he was slightly foolish. Somewhat of a clown by nature, Phillip would stroll through Rome wearing his clothes inside out along with floppy white shoes to amuse those who stared at him, to dispel the idea that saints should be solemn.

When Phillip heard people were impressed by his humble ways, he thought of borrowing a friend's mink cloak. Thus robed he appeared in public, posturing vainly and acting like a snob. He seemed to enjoy upsetting popular expectations about saintliness, especially those stuffy perceptions that were common in his own day. The child in Phillip found mischievous ways to achieve his goal, such as occasionally shaving only half his beard, or strutting around with a large blue cushion perched on his head.

Is this what saints would ever do? Is this how a friend of Popes, cardinals, princes and all the "powers that be" would behave? Phillip did because he wanted to cause a shock of recognition of his humanity, and to show that holiness was far more akin to laughter and love than to self-conscious seriousness or identity with the mighty.

Phillip found hundreds of ways to undermine pretentiousness, both in himself and his followers. He might arrive at church wearing an old jacket over his cassock, his biretta cocked on the side of his head, accompanied by a friend instructed to keep brushing off nonexistent lint from his clothes. When pompous clergy came to dine with him, Phillip entertained them by bringing out a monkey wearing a biretta and carrying a gun. Once when an overly-awed party of Polish noblemen arrived for a visit, Phillip kept them waiting while he read out loud some jokes from a humor book by Mainardi, the Florentine satirist. After a few good laughs, Phillip said to them, "You see how important are the issues that claim my attention."

Responding to an ascetic impulse, a disciple of Phillip's asked permission to wear a hair shirt. With unsuppressed amusement, Phillip agreed wholeheartedly, "Yes you may have your hair shirt. But you must wear it outside your coat and not next to your skin." The man had not expected this embarrassment which far exceeded the self-congratulatory plan he originally had in mind. Phillip judged correctly that an itch to one's feelings may well be a greater mortification than bodily discomfort.

Phillip was an enthusiastic enemy of vanity. Listening to the eloquent sermon of one of his newly ordained priests, he sensed the young man was just a little too full of his own self-importance. Phillip deflated that attitude by ordering the man to give the same sermon on the following six Sundays. By the last week people were saying, "Here comes the one-sermon priest." Because of Phillip's basic good humor, he was able to correct this man without breaking him, and the young man learned how to be eloquent without going on an ego trip.

This cheerful and insightful mystic, Phillip Neri, was born in Florence of a middle-class family. In his youth he was personally impressed by the career of the Florentine Dominican reformer, Savanorala, who was burned at the stake a generation before. Phillip's parents had arranged for him to become a businessman, but he felt drawn to religious ministry. Rejecting a future in business, Phillip moved to Rome where he served as a tutor to earn a living, while he completed a three-year course of studies in philosophy and theology.

Instead of seeking ordination to the priesthood, the twenty-one-year-old Phillip embarked on a thirteen-year career as a lay minister in Rome. Luther's Reformation was in full swing. Rome was a city of lazy priests, corrupt Church officials and a paganized laity. The Council of Trent that would spur the Counter-Reformation was only just beginning. Rome needed to reform the Church. But someone had to reform Rome. Phillip Neri, destined to be known as the "Second Apostle of Rome," would become the spiritual architect of the reform of Rome, bringing his formidable spiritual presence and influence to bear on the power elite of Rome for the next fifty-nine years of his life.

It all began slowly and simply enough. Inwardly, Phillip felt an intense drive to contemplative prayer, to which he devoted substantial time each day. Over the years his prayer assumed the qualities of mystical depth, and occasionally an attraction so intense he could scarcely keep himself from withdrawing into the all-absorbing joy of the experience. He was later to testify that this was another reason he opted for silly clowning around, because that helped him retain his self-possession at Eucharist, as well as when he needed it for active outreach.

His active lay ministry included the traditional works of charity for the poor and the deprived. With some friends he built a hospital for cash-poor pilgrims. After thirteen years in this ministry, he accepted the call to priesthood, in which he continued his previous commitment to prayer and good works, but now added a dedication to Confessional ministry and that of continuing education.

Phillip used the confessional both for spiritual counseling as well as the forgiveness of sins. He followed this up with afternoon seminars and institutes on the bible, spiritual life, Church history and the lives of the saints. There would normally be four sessions of speeches and discussions, interspersed with prayer and music. These sessions were held in an *Oratory* or prayer room.

Possessed of an instinctive love of quality music and appreciative of the value of singing to promote group enthusiasm and cohesiveness, Phillip attracted some of the best musicians of Rome to his Oratory. He encouraged them to compose hymns, songs, and madrigals based on dramatic stories from the bible, such as the dialogue of Jesus with the Woman at the Well. Phillip insisted that many of the lyrics be in Italian so that the meaning was immediately clear to his people. He also asked them to write in simple melodic lines to make sure that the words could be heard as well as understood.

At that time, Church music was in just as sorry a state as doctrine, discipline and morality. One was liable to hear hymns that were nothing more than sentimental love songs, allusively erotic, with no reference to Christ or any divine meaning. At other times one might hear hymns, whether humanistic or divine, submerged by deafening organs and drums, so that the texts could not be heard. Some Popes, frustrated by this musical mess, were about to eliminate all music from Churches, but settled for banning the totally humanistic songs.

In Phillip's Oratory, musical geniuses such as Animuccia and Palestrina began the rejuvenation of Church music, creating the "Renaissance Polyphony" that has become one of the glories of ecclesiastical music. And in their musical, vernacular settings of the dramatic dialogues of the bible, they created the "musical plays" that evolved into works such as Handel's "Messiah" and Haydn's "Creation" and Bach's "St. Matthew's Passion." The *Oratorios* of the great Protestant master musicians started in the Catholic *Oratory* of Phillip Neri, and it is from his prayer room that the name and style of that musical form originated. Phillip may have acted like a fool to cool the temperatures of the saint seekers, but he was no fool when it came to being a person of superb musical taste.

Nor did he play the idiot when it was a matter of fostering scholarship. His Oratory was a sacred salon for truth seekers, among whom was a brilliant historian, Caesar Baronius. The Catholicism of the time was in sore need of an updated, factual history of the Church. Too much of the available history was a hodge-podge of legends, biased asides and just plain inaccuracies. Baronius delivered well researched Church history talks each afternoon and refined his presentations through the lively exchange that followed his talks. Out of this grew the many volumes of his *Ecclesiastical History* that remains to this day a model of scholarly writing.

Gradually Phillip was prevailed upon to create a religious institute out of his major followers and disciples. They lived as a religious community at the Church of the Florentines. Though they took no vows, they did have a loose fitting organization that proved to be successful in the years to come. This Congregation of the Oratory, or the Oratorians, was to boast Cardinal Newman of England as one of its most prominent members. As they grew in Rome they moved to the run-down parish of St. Maria in Vallicella, where they built a new Church and community house. Today it is still called Chiesa Nuova—"New Church."

Over the years Phillip became the confidante and spiritual counselor to a dizzying number of ecclesiastical VIP's—Ignatius Loyola, Francis de Sales, Camillus de Lellis, Charles Borromeo (all to become canonized saints), not to mention an assorted list of Popes, cardinals, bishops and generals of religious orders. His appealing personality, expert skills as a spiritual adviser and sheer longevity (died at eighty) had much to do with his remarkable influence.

A final, passing note is deserved about "Phillip's Picnics." He was annoyed by the restoration of the Mardi Gras in Rome, in whose carnival atmosphere gross and debasing amusements eroded the moral character of the participants. To counteract the carnival parade, Phillip invented the Christian parade to the Seven Churches, the principal basilicas of Rome. The daylong journey was marked by prayers, talks, discussions, music by Palestrina and Animuccia and stops for food—picnics, accompanied by party-like banter and singing. These entertaining pilgrimages became so popular that the thousands who wanted to join in them were divided up into smaller units with assigned leaders, and with Phillip doing his best to rush from one group to another to greet and encourage them. His picnics were another case of his charming ability to light candles, rather than curse the darkness, a uniquely positive feature of his lifelong ministry.

While active until his final days, Phillip was more and more drawn into the absorption of prayer and love for Christ. He died in his eightieth year, having evangelized the saved by calling them to a conversion to holiness.

He was canonized in 1622 along with Ignatius and Teresa.

Reflection

Phillip retained, throughout all his life, an extreme distaste for personal honors. He virtually acted as though he were not the official head of the Oratorians and was more than wily about staving off repeated attempts by the Popes to make him a Cardinal. When one Pope left the Cardinal's hat in his room, Phillip proceeded to insist on playing catch with it as though it were a ball. Phillip was never loathe to assume leadership duties so long as he could exercise them with personal authority. He resolutely rejected any attempt to clothe him in official or institutional aspects of leadership. In modern terms Phillip was almost a pure "personalist," whose prayer shot him to the heavens and whose humor welded him to earth. Small wonder he has been called so correctly, "The Patriarch of the Counter Reformation."

Rose of Lima

(1586–1617)

She Faced Down Inquisitors and Pirates

"Without service there is no grace. Let no one be mistaken, this is the heavenly measure of one's life."
Rose, An Account of Her Visions

While the Catholic Church of the sixteenth century was losing some ground to Henry VIII and Luther, it gained a strong foothold in Latin America by means of the Spanish and Portuguese colonial conquests. As Reform and Counter-Reform theologians battled over doctrine and discipline, Catholic missionaries flowed across the Atlantic with Papal and royal mandates to evangelize the New World.

In Mexico they found the civilized Aztecs and in Peru the cultured Incas, both countries possessing large Indian populations who lived an ordered life built around a settled agriculture. Within a generation after the arrival of Columbus to America, a small handful of Spaniards had replaced the ruling elites in Mexico and Peru. Outward acceptance of Christianity occurred fairly rapidly among these people who capitulated, as they generally had before, to their new masters.

One may not ignore the fact that this was accomplished by violence and war, and that the conquest was partly motivated, as most military aggression is, by greed. Nevertheless, the official policy of Spain and Portugal stated that a purpose for conquering the New World was the conversion of the Indians to Christ. The sword of the Conquistador would be accompanied by the Cross of the missionary.

The main center of Spanish colonial power in South America was Peru. Only forty-three years after the discovery of America, Pizarro had completed the conquest of Peru and founded the city of Lima in 1535. In a short time, the city acquired all the trappings of a city of power, elegance and culture, with its government buildings, monasteries, theaters and great homes.

It was here that Rose de Flores was born in 1586, sired by a veteran Conquistador, Gaspar de Flores and Maria de Oliva, a woman whose mother was almost certainly an Inca. Though the baby was baptized Isabel, her pink complexion moved the family to call her Rose, and that name stuck.

The man who baptized her was the remarkable missionary Archbishop of Lima, Toribio Robles. In Spain he had enjoyed the privilege of wealth and education, but in mid-life he experienced a religious conversion, applied for the priesthood and journeyed to Peru as a missionary. He took the time to learn the Inca language (known as Quechua) and study the culture of the Inca peoples. As Archbishop he lived an austere life, traveled extensively on foot all over his diocese where, it is said, he confirmed literally hundreds of thousands of his people. He built roads, schools, chapels and hospitals and instituted policies in defense of the Indians and the religious rights of the black slaves.

Rose received baptism from this courageous missionary on the feast of Pentecost. The young Rose proved to be a determined girl with a mind of her own. She was much taken with the life of Catherine of Siena and admired the independent spirit of that woman. Like Catherine she decided early in life that she would not marry and that she would devote herself to prayer and good works. The records of the time report that Rose was a beauty, so that her desire to remain celibate posed a challenge for her. Men were understandably attracted to her and her parents saw no reason why she should not marry.

During her adolescent years, Rose firmly withstood all efforts to match her with a husband. She argued that she wanted to be a cloistered nun and made several fruitless efforts to enter one or another of the convents of Lima. Her parents stubbornly opposed her becoming a nun. Remembering her role model, Catherine of Siena, Rose sought and received a membership in the Third Order of St. Dominic. For the rest of her life she would live the rules of cloister as a laywoman in the world of Lima.

As Catherine had once found a room for herself in the noisy household of Siena, so Rose built a hermitage for herself on the family property. Though her family was middle class, it was perennially short of money. Her father's military income was supplemented by her mother's salary as a teacher. Rose felt a responsibility to help with the family finances needed to cover the raising of eight children and the upkeep of the property. Rose discovered she had a green thumb, not a bad talent in the favorable gardening climate of Lima. Though the city borders on the Pacific Ocean, it is technically a desert since the surrounding Andes mountains close out virtually all rainfall. But it responds well to irrigation. Rose devoted a portion of each day to the garden and developed a flower business, whose income appeased her parents' displeasure with their strange daughter.

They were less pleased, and equally helpless, when the ever determined Rose took over a room in the house for an infirmary for the poor. It is quite likely that Rose learned about herbal medicine from her Inca grandmother, a training that would be augmented by her gardening skills. Rose was in tune with nature as well as with God. She also realized the need to serve the deprived who began flocking to her makeshift clinic. Official records credit her with initiating social services in Peru. Medical services did exist in the Lima of the time. As a matter of fact the prominent Holy Spirit hospital bordered the property of Rose's household. What was needed was free medical service for the poor, and this is what Rose offered. Like Schweitzer of Africa and Teresa of India, Rose raised the awareness of people to the needs of the poor.

It is a pity, however, that we have so little information about that aspect of Rose's life. Her biographers seemed far more fascinated by her mortifications of the flesh than her service to the poor. They appear to have an almost morose interest in the fact that she wore a pewter cap, lined with small thorns and hidden by her Dominican Tertiary veil. Rose's mother was repelled by this behavior. Rose soothed her mother by tucking fresh roses each day on her veil. Rose also locked an iron belt around her waist and threw the key in a well. She took to scourging herself with a chain. In time the belt was removed and the scourging abandoned, but only after Rose was convinced that her passions were under control and her mystical union with Christ a matter of stability and growth.

The members of the Inquisition, always nervous about deviance from Catholic orthodoxy and perennially worried about the independent spirit of noted mystics, decided they had better look into the case of Rose de Flores. Mercifully, they did not bring her to the intimidating chambers of the Inquisition, but arranged an investigation at her home, permitting her mother and Rose's closest friend, Dona Maria, to sit with her for support. Rose was questioned by a medical doctor and a theology professor.

It is difficult to know what kind of woman these men expected to find. They saw a woman of considerable beauty and may have been disarmed by the feminine touches, such as the fresh roses arranged on her veil. They would have no way of knowing this was a woman seasoned by years of prayer and self-discipline, and toughened by her garden work and physical efforts at the infirmary. They found out very quickly that Rose was no wilting recluse. She showed no signs of being intimidated, far from it as she spoke to them from reserves of assurance and confidence that probably put them a bit on the defensive.

They wanted to know what books on mystical prayer she had studied and who had been her trainer in the ways of prayer. She told them that she could read, but seldom did so, and had never heard of the textbooks on prayer. She made it clear to them that she was a self-made woman on the matter of prayer. From her earliest years she had felt the tug to center herself in Christ and she had willingly surrendered to that impulse. If she had any external spiritual influence, it was the example of her beloved Catherine of Siena. Internally, her spiritual teacher was Christ who drew her each day more deeply to the divine. The members of the Inquisition tested her understanding of the major Christian doctrines and heard her give forthright, orthodox and convincing explanations of the issues. As one reads the report of these investigators, the impression arises that Rose was an imposing witness. She had so convinced them of the authenticity of her life that when she admitted, at their prodding, that yes she had visions of Christ, they believed her without reserve. The investigators concluded that no charges could be lodged against Rose, for she was evidently acting under the impulse of grace.

Perhaps the event that drew the greatest amount of popular attention to Rose was her role in saving Lima from the devastation of the Dutch pirate, Jorge Spitberg. Apparently the last of the great pirates in the tradition of Drake, Cavendish and Hawkins, Spitberg had broken through a Peruvian naval blockade and began bombarding Lima. A detachment of his sailors had forced their way through the Lima militia with a mandate to plunder the cathedral where the children and women—including Rose—had gone for safety.

Rose had made up her mind that she would struggle to defend somehow the women and children from whatever these nautical gangsters intended. She also was determined to protect the treasures of the Cathedral. It is not at all clear what actually happened, since no detailed account of the event exists. All we know is that when the sailors crashed through the Cathedral door, they were forced to cope with Rose and her personal forcefulness. Whether she bargained, commanded, cajoled, or simply faced them down with an irresistible spiritual power, the fact of the matter seems to be they left Lima unmolested due to the intervention of Rose de Flores.

With this, Rose became the most celebrated person in Lima, always loved by the poor and now worshipped as a living saint by the people at large. None of the adulation turned her head as she continued her prayer, work in the infirmary, and flower business. In her thirtieth year, her health declined rapidly and brought about her death on Aug. 24, 1617. A religious hysteria swept the mourning crowds for the next three days, as they sought to view the saint and touch her body. She was quietly buried in St. Dominic's cloister as she had requested.

Clement X officiated at her canonization in 1671.

Reflection

Rose of Lima comes across as a woman who knew how to be flexible on negotiable issues and absolute about the non-negotiable ones, such as her privacy, prayer, asceticism and work in her infirmary. Here we have an ascetic who runs a flower business to help support her family and a mystic employing her skills as a herbalist to heal the poor in her infirmary. As a gardener and a nurse she appeared to lead a low-keyed life, for a woman of her time. But in her precious hermitage, she built up a capacity for prayer that released a tremendous sense of God awareness in Peru. Columbus discovered a new world. Rose discovered a very old one. For that she became America's first saint.

Peter Claver

(1581–1654)

The Blacks Knew He Loved Them

"We must speak to them with our hands, before we try to speak to them with our lips."

Peter Claver, Maxims

Modern Cartagena shimmers with all the glamorous luxury of a Caribbean resort. Four hundred years ago, it shuddered with the gut-wrenching yells of a continuous stream of slave ships bearing over ten thousand blacks a year to its slave markets. One may notice there today a dark, weathered statue of a Jesuit named Peter Claver. Originally, it had been white marble, but was darkened by the salt air. Popular tradition says that the black people noted this change with knowing glances, claiming, "Father Claver must have been a black, for a white man would never have loved us so much."

When Peter arrived in Cartagena as a thirty-one-year-old Spanish Jesuit seminarian, he was not yet aware of the special mission to which he would be called. Once there, however, he could scarcely ignore the fact that the all absorbing purpose of the city was the importing and merchandising of black slaves. Slave ships in the harbor. Slave warehouses within the city limits. Public slave markets. Hotels full of prospective purchasers, offices teeming with accountants and salespersons and bargaining agents. Peter Claver was entering a hell hole of inhumanity, an inferno of cruelty.

At the same time he encountered massive denial and culturally enforced indifference to this institutionalized exploitation of human beings. He had never seen slaves in Spain. He had heard that Pope Paul III had condemned the practice of slavery. Now he was to note that slavery was so bound up with the economic well-being and future of Cartagena and its clients that little attention was paid to its immorality. The people had made an ethical compromise in order to be prosperous, so they lived easily with their consciences.

Fortunately for the blacks, there was one Jesuit who had not numbed his social conscience by accepting the self-serving rationalizations of the Christian community of Cartagena. For forty years, the Jesuit Alonso de Sandoval went against this tide of massive indifference. He was sharp enough to see that it would be hopeless to insist on the abolition of slavery at this point. The groundwork must be laid that would raise the awareness of people to see the humanity of the slaves and thus to treat them with justice and kindness. Sandoval realized that he must settle for the modest goal of humane treatment and then hope that the systemic injustice itself would eventually be wiped out.

This was one reason why he worked so hard to baptize the slaves in the Christian faith. Of course he believed in the importance of offering the slaves the possibility of salvation in Christ and felt strongly that faith in Jesus would enable them to bear their indignities with a spiritual motivation. His strategy also included the assumption that presenting the slave as a Christian to the owner, would give the slave title to being perceived as a human person and thus deserving of decent treatment. This was a slow and subtle process that would take years to implement, but one which did eventually succeed.

Sandoval found in Peter Claver a superb successor to carry on his plan and fulfill his vision. Carefully tutoring Peter in his philosophy of evangelization and training him in the appropriate conversion methods, Sandoval created a disciple who would enthusiastically surpass the master. Peter Claver studied Sandoval's classic treatises describing the history of the slave trade, the ethnology of the blacks and the methods for evangelization. From the moment of his ordination at thirty-six, Claver never deviated from absolute and loving dedication to the blacks who flooded the port of Cartagena. For the next forty years he would serve them, as he said, as the "slave of the slaves."

Claver assimilated Sandoval's fundamental admonition to treat the blacks as persons, as humans deserving of respect, and therefore not animals to be beaten as dogs and horses or starved into submission as if they were sub-humans. Peter's ministry would be a visible sermon in human rights, operating from the principle, "If you treat the blacks as humans, then you will begin to believe in their humanity." This was the astute consciousness raising behind the strenuous efforts to baptize as many of the blacks as possible. It was a prophetic protest against the prevailing psychological denial that would consider the blacks to be merely animals.

It is important to keep this in mind when examining the ministry of Peter Claver because there could easily be an impatience today that would try to impose upon the seventeenth century, in keeping with our view of human rights, the advancements made by civil rights movements. The essential kernel of modern enlightenment was there, but their history was not ready for the radical systemic change that even in modern America has not reached the maturity it should, as becomes clear in the wake of Alex Haley's "Roots" and the continued need for CORE and the NAACP.

As Claver boarded the slave ships or roamed through the slave warehouses and stockyards, he proceeded with the conviction that he was dealing with human beings who required tenderness, love, affection and salvation. From the rich people of Cartagena, Claver begged medicines, food, bread, brandy, lemons, clothing and tobacco.

Sandoval had trained him to recognize the ethnic differences he would meet. Moving among them he could hear Sandoval's expert descriptions.

"The Popos are marked by a bow and arrows, encircling their temples on both sides, the arrows coming from the sides of their eyes toward the ears. . . . The Ardas have a variety of marks. Some have a band across their temples of a different color from their faces. Others have three or four deep lines on their faces below their eyes which give them a certain beauty. . . . The Lucumies pierce the left nostril without having any other mark. . . . Knowing these distinctions will help you pick the right interpreters and greatly console these people with your recognition."

Claver must have been a man of enormous energy, for witnesses verify he met and baptized about 300,000 blacks over a forty-year ministry. This is not only a matter of numbers, but also of the strain to communicate in a variety of languages, of physical effort exerted to carry literally thousands of sick blacks to comfort areas for treatment, of fighting back the urge to vomit when assailed by the odors of the slave holds, of enduring the tensions caused by the hostile slave marketers, of the lifelong frustration of knowing how slowly the lesson of charity and justice was being learned.

Claver's method of evangelization had its human and sacramental components. The human phase involved meeting the blacks, showing recognition for their ethnic origins and welcoming them with gifts and hugs—and fresh water, both for drinking and for washing after their dreadful voyage. This phase also involved taking care of their sick. For this purpose Claver had studied medicine as well as theology. One gathers that Claver must have been a good organizer, because he only had about one month to deal with a thousand slaves before they went onto the plantations in distant places. Yet within this month he seemed able to meet most of them and set up the catechesis, through interpreters, that would prepare them for the sacraments.

Almost certainly Claver's therapy of kindness had a great deal to do with his incredible success as an evangelizer. A warm-hearted man, he went about easily hugging, loving, feeding, dosing and caring for these hordes of frightened people. He was the first, and probably only, kind white man they met since leaving Africa. In the midst of all their misery he must have seemed a veritable angel convincing them that love and hope were still possible. When he finally invited them to the waters of Baptism, they found his appeal irresistible. The man who had slaked their thirst and helped wash their bodies with clean water now offered them the waters of salvation for their spirit. By the tens of thousands they approached this marvelous man who had convinced them that he believed in their personal dignity and had restored in them a sense of self-worth nearly destroyed by the wretched trauma of the previous months.

They could not avoid physical captivity, but they found a way to inner spiritual freedom through a Baptism in the name of the Father, Son and Holy Spirit. They also knew, as he instructed them, that they had a claim upon the consciences of their masters for decent treatment as Christian human beings. More deeply, they could in the decades to come mount a movement that would bring about their liberation from slavery altogether. Peter Claver was planting a dream in the slaves of Cartagena, a spiritual basis for the political and economic independence that would come later.

In the light of all this, one wonders where Claver found time for anything else, such as prayer or the moral enlightenment sermons he gave regularly to the sailors in the town square and the ruling class in the local churches. But find time he did. All the records show that he spent hours in contemplation each day, asserting that the love and energy that he was able to expend flowed from this prayerful contact with Christ. He considered his daily centering in Christ to be the absolute pre-requisite for his mission to the blacks.

Like any public figure, whether saint or otherwise, Claver was bound to be misunderstood and sometimes opposed. In his forty years he lived under ten different superiors who had twenty-four other Jesuits to think about. They were not always sympathetic to his ministry. Nor were the people at the Jesuit parish happy when Peter would fill the place with his "smelly" slaves. And clearly the barons of the slave trade were never happy with him. The marvel is how well he got along anyhow.

Remarkably, the ones who defended Peter most were the top Jesuit superiors. Here are some of their opinions:

1616. Mental powers, less than mediocre. Prudence, lacking. Character, easily moved to anger. Ability for mission work, useful for hearing confessions and dealing with the natives.

1651. Mental powers, good. Prudence, lacking. Ability in mission work, good. Advance in spiritual matters, excellent.

Odd is it not that they judged this man who knew Greek, Latin, and held degrees in philosophy and theology as having little intellectual competence—good at best. They were using continuing scholarship as a norm for a man ministering to a thousand slaves a month. Still their report was positive for the most part. Claver did not seem too worried. He loved his blacks and served them as long as his strength held out.

Claver died on September 8, 1654. The hostile city fathers gave him the equivalent of a State Funeral. The Church canonized him in 1888.

Reflection

Claver took the vision and scholarship of Sandoval and gave these a concrete realization that remains a record of heroism and courage. His ingenious combination of the human and the sacramental is a method of evangelization that still seems fresh and new today. He dealt with injustice as well as he could. May the record of our own history prove to be as inspiring.

Angela Merici

(1470–1540)

A Champion of Educational Rights for Women

"If according to times and needs you should be obliged to make fresh rules and change certain things, do it with prudence and on good advice."

Rule of St. Angela

If a medieval woman wanted an education, she would either have to be rich or be a nun. Since there were thousands of convents in that period, and given the fact that these cloisters were centers of formal education, one may conclude that a considerable number of medieval women were well educated. In fact one of the surviving sayings of the time is, "Education is for women and clerics."

With the passing of the middle ages and the coming of the modern era, some method was needed to help educate the general population of women beyond those who were rich or cloistered. The solution was created by an inventive Italian woman, Angela Merici. Born in Desenzano, Venice, she spent the first fifty-six years of her life as a kind of lay contemplative. A member of the Third Order of St. Francis, she passed her days in prayer and good works.

In 1516 she was invited to Brescia by the Patengoli family, to keep them company and console them in the wake of the death of their two sons. As the years went by she found herself growing sensitive to the needs of the deprived girls of the city. She judged that their lack of education put them at a disadvantage and began to ponder some way to help them.

The only available model for educating women was that found in the cloisters, though there were also tutors and governesses for the rich women. The girls who claimed her attention could never afford tutors and were not drawn to enter the cloister. The nuns of the day were not permitted to go out among the people, except in cases of emergency, such as helping the plague victims.

It was in her fifty-seventh year that Angela hit upon the idea of forming a group of like-minded women, interested in the education of young girls, who would join together for that purpose. They would be nuns without habits, sisters living in their own homes, consecrated virgins dedicated to the educational ministry. Thus Angela Merici founded what we call today a *secular institute* in 1535.

Angela assembled twenty-eight like-minded women and created the "Company of St. Ursula," or the Ursulines as they would come to be known. She chose St. Ursula because of her connection with education as patroness of the medieval universities, and also because of her role as a leader of women. The Ursulines became the first group of women religious to seek a form of religious life outside the traditional cloister model that had prevailed until that time.

Male religious orders had begun to seek noncloistered forms of religious life four centuries before. In 1120 St. Norbert endeavored to create a system where cloistered living would be combined with active ministry to the world. The Dominicans and Franciscans devised an even more explicit activist ministry in the thirteenth century. The Jesuits brought an aggressive individualism to active ministry in the sixteenth century. By then non-cloistered forms of ministry for male religious had become an accepted norm, even as the traditional Benedictine and Cistercian cloistered life maintained its historic approach.

Angela could only hope to succeed in such a venture because the culture somewhat favored a liberated view of women in society. Such must have been the case in sixteenth-century Brescia. The idea of single, unmarried women—even if they be nuns—moving into the towns and cities to minister to the ignorant, sick and downtrodden may seem commonplace to us. It was a new idea then, and one for which the Company of St. Ursula is to be commended.

Perhaps one feature that fostered acceptance for Angela Merici's novel concept was the clear need for reform in the Church and the growing acceptance of plans to do something about it. Strong sentiments for a Counter-Reformation were sweeping through the Church, led by the vital work of Phillip Neri, Ignatius Loyla and Teresa of Avila. The semi-paganism that had become a way of life in Renaissance Italy needed the counter-cultural response of re-Christianizing the family. Angela believed that the cornerstone of Christian values in the family was the woman as wife and mother. From her would radiate the direction and nourishment that could remake the Christian family. In other words, "Convert the woman and one converts the family."

The instrument Angela chose for doing this was religious education. She and her Company of St. Ursula would teach young women how to read and write, giving them the basic tools of learning, and showing them how to continue their personal growth throughout their lives. Education was the means and Christian living was the goal. Even though religion was the core content of the curriculum, Angela insisted on mastery of learning skills and opened up to her students the possibility of engaging in other branches of learning. She was taking women, otherwise destined to be illiterate, and transmitting to them an access to the world of learning. She encountered superstitious, half pagans and produced for them the condition for the possibility of becoming conscious and committed Christians.

For the last fourteen years of her life, Angela developed and refined her approach. She developed a series of rules whereby her sisters would live. Flexibility was built into her Rule. "If according to times and needs you should be obliged to make fresh rules and change certain things, do it with patience and on good advice." While education was her primary interest, she permitted her sisters to follow their ministerial instincts. Many of them held classes in their homes. Others worked at their parish centers. Some followed their nursing inclinations and served in the hospitals, choosing as a specialized ministry a service to those afflicted with venereal disease.

Time was to be set aside each day for prayer. They met together at least once a month for a day of prayer and a discussion of their ministry, reflecting on their experiences and fine tuning their approaches. The Brescia Sisters created a movement in Christian education that was to prove of enormous benefit for women as well as men in the centuries to come, witnessed by the dozens of teaching orders of Sisters that were to follow them and implement their vision.

The succeeding years brought about a modification of their lifestyle, though never snuffing out their vision. Forty years after their founding, Archbishop Charles Borromeo asked the Sisters to live together in convent communities, rather than in their own homes. They also gradually began to adopt a distinctive habit. In the year 1700—165 years from the date of founding—a large group of the Ursulines decided to live in cloister as a condition for being recognized as nuns in the Church. They did not, however, abandon Angela's dream of public and active ministry. To this end, they insisted on taking a fourth vow—that of teaching—so that they would have an active apostolate, even though it was within the walls of a cloister.

They remained inventive in finding ways to do active work for the Church. The Ursulines of New Orleans, for example, established in 1727 the first Catholic school in what would be continental United States. They characterized their school as a hostel for marriageable women and stated they would teach these women "all they needed to know" about marriage and the care of a Christian home. They even produced an "Ursuline Cook Book" (What else in New Oreans?). So involved were they in the history of New Orleans, that the 250th anniversary of their coming to the city was feted by the city fathers as a major civic event. And so "worldly" were these cloistered nuns and their concerns that they sent a letter to President Jefferson confiding their worries about the Louisiana Purchase. They feared that the purchase of Louisiana by a Protestant country would bring with it prejudice and bigotry against Catholics, and the possible termination of their work. Jefferson assured them that their fears were groundless. They would have the freedom they sought.

In the updating of women's religious orders since Vatican II, the Ursulines have shed the restrictions of cloister once again, as Angela Merici originally intended. They have remained faithful to their commitment to Christian education. They still live in community, and not in their homes as the original Sisters did.

Angela Merici could respond to a crying need of her culture because the mood of reform favored her idea. Another element that created a welcome for her vision was the gospel of the humanists such as More and Erasmus. They were convinced that education was an instrument of social reform and religious reform as well. The enlightenment of the mind would make spiritual enlightenment more possible. An educated intelligence would be more apt to lead to desired moral behavior. The impetus which the Christian humanists gave to education fostered the acceptance of formal learning as a key element in the revitalization of the Church. The Jesuits vigorously implemented this ideal with their vast network of colleges for men.

It took the courage and insight of an old Italian lady in Brescia to see that women deserved every bit as much. In the twentieth century another Italian woman, Maria Montessori, felt a similar compassion for the young and deprived women of the city of Rome. She, too, saw education as a key to releasing the human potential of the poor children of her city—boys as well as girls. She did not found a religious order, but she did create a new and humane method of teaching, widely used throughout the world. Angela, doubtless, would be pleased, as she would also delight in the fact that today an educated woman is an expected and accepted fact of life.

The Church canonized Angela Merici on May 24, 1807.

Reflection

It was the genius of Angela Merici that stood up for the rights of women to get an education outside the traditional cloister walls. She realized that one need not live in a cloister or go to one in order to have an education. She was even more daring—inventing a new kind of nun—for she upheld the ideals of religious celibacy, poverty and obedience as a woman's right, and this lifestyle need not be protected by a cloister's walls. She created a form of Sisterhood that was to produce the greatest form of private education in history, a private education made available not just to the rich, but also to the poor. She was an innovator in the best sense of the word, a champion of women's rights, and a benefactor to all who seek a Christian education.

Francis de Sales

(1567–1622)

He Saw the Value of the Print Medium

"Divine love not only commands us again and again to love our neighbor, but itself produces the love as its own image and likeness and shed it over our hearts."
Francis de Sales, Treatise on the Love of God

In the narrow streets of Padua's university district a small group of students prepared to ambush and haze a young man whose quiet and studious ways at the law school aroused their envy and their distaste. It was a perfect setup for bullies and their hapless victim. The young man proved to be a superb foil, if one may use a pun, for he turned out to be a skilled swordsman who put them on the defensive and chased them away, probably with a good laugh.

Apparently they were unaware that Francis de Sales was a trained fencer. They might also have been surprised to know that he was an expert horseman and a smooth man on the dance floor. By the time Francis had come to Padua, he had resolved to be a celibate and was beginning to think of priesthood, therefore his dating skills and martial talents were put aside in view of his new goals.

The oldest of thirteen children, Francis as the first-born son occupied a privileged place in his household.

His father wanted Francis to replace him as a senator in the government of Savoy, making sure that he had the requisite classics training and a degree in law.

Francis disappointed his father by firmly and stubbornly refusing a career in politics, choosing instead to be a priest. While depressed by his son's decision, the father was partially consoled that Francis would be named to the prestigious post of Dean of St. Peter's Church in Geneva—some strings having been pulled by an influential cousin. Bishop Claude de Granier ordained Francis to the priesthood on December 18, 1593.

Those were the days when religion was a political football between Protestants and Catholics. The region of Savoy was a battleground for Calvinists and Catholics and the shifting tides of wars saw a game of musical chairs, one time the Catholics winning, another time, the Calvinists. If a Calvinist leader won, he attempted to force all the citizens to follow his faith, likewise a victorious Catholic leader would strive to bring the Calvinists back to Rome.

This was the see-saw, religio-political world in which Francis de Sales would pursue his priestly ministry. The axiom of the day was "Cuius regio, eius religio," which paraphrased means that the religion of the people should follow the religion of the king. The newly ordained Francis began his priestly career with the freshly victorious Catholic Duke of Savoy. Missionary priests were needed especially in the state of Chablis on the south shore of Lake Geneva, populated mostly by convinced Calvinists. Political pressure would not be enough to force these people to become Catholics. A systematic and vigorous evangelization was more than necessary.

Francis followed the traditional tactic of moving from town to town, visiting Catholic families to encourage them, while using their homes as bases for outreach to Calvinists. Francis found this process slow, inefficient and frustrating. Not enough people were being touched on a regular and persuasive basis. Worrying through this problem, Francis discovered what Luther had already known and mastered, namely, the power of the print medium to spread ideas, change minds and convert people.

Francis became a pamphleteer, taking advantage of a communications medium that had been around for over a century, but scarcely used at all by the Church to implement its mission. He began writing what amounted to a weekly newsletter, containing a point of Catholic doctrine in simple and lucid prose, along with arguments against the Calvinist positions. For the first few months, he experimented with the idea having copies produced by hand. When he saw how successful the handwritten materials were, he then moved to print.

This was the beginning of his career as a religious journalist and the main reason why he is today the patron saint of journalism. In realizing the power of the printed word, Francis evolved into a propagandist for Catholicism in the best sense of that word. Since he could never hope to be physically present to so many thousands of people on a regular and consistent basis, he did the next best thing, he came to them in pamphlets, books and letters. In our world, gorged by the print medium, this may seem a self-evident strategy, but then it was a new idea. For now the printing press was not just an instrument for reproducing the works of the past, it could serve as an instrument for evangelization for the newly literate populations in the middle-class urban centers.

In addition Francis found within himself another unsuspected talent, that he happened to be an unusually appealing public speaker. His training in classics supplied him with the abundant imagery of the poets and his years at law school taught him the arts of persuasion. But he was unique in his decision to use a low-key, laid-back speaking style so much in contrast to the pretentious fulminations of the accepted preaching style of the day. Francis had the common touch and a sure sense of where his audience was, as well as a poet's gift for choosing down-home comparisons, as is evident in his often-quoted advice about motivation, "that a spoonful of honey works far better than a barrel of vinegar." Actually, his conversational speaking style is the kind looked for in today's TV presenters, relaxed and natural, pungent without being pugnacious, a capacity to be critical of an opposition without being too shrill or strident.

He delivered thousands of sermons in this manner in hundreds of cities and towns, knowing instinctively that when the audience has seen and heard the speaker, the follow-up pamphlets and books will make more sense. The calmness of his speaking style and the sweet reasonableness of his soft-sell approach have led many commentators to speak mellifluously of the "gentle de Sales." This is a misleading characterization, for it implies that Francis leaned to the sentimental. His was a gentleness only by contrast to the angry polemicism and theatrical posturing that prevailed in those days. Francis was far more of a contained volcano than a flowing pitcher of syrup. He was a brilliant, disciplined stylist whose writings to this day serve as an example of French prose. He was a self-assured speaker who resolutely repudiated power plays against his audience because he believed in their inner capacity to hear the truth and come to faith.

Francis believed passionately in the power of the laity to serve as evangelizers for the faith. It was this conviction that moved him to write a masterpiece of spiritual growth in a language immediately available to the laity, "The Introduction To a Devout Life." Written in an uncomplicated prose, this book offers systematic and sensible advice on how to meditate, how to develop a Christian value-oriented character and to surrender oneself to the impulses of grace. He possessed a genius for writing about mysticism without sounding mysterious, thereby making available for millions of laity the kind of spiritual insight once reserved to cloisters. So successful has this work and his "Treatise on the Love of God" (written for the nuns of the Visitation Order) been on the consciousness of following generations, that they have become the core literature of what is known as "The Salesian School of Spirituality." They also account for Rome's naming Francis a Doctor of the Church.

By creating a trained laity in the arts of spirituality, and therefore open to evangelizing, Francis again multiplied his effectiveness just as he had through the use of print. He had no messiah complex that would reserve all conversion efforts to his own personal presence. He relied on the power of God's presence working through the printed word and in the converted lives of the thousands of laity influenced by his spiritual insights.

At the same time Francis understood the value of being open and available to people. When he became the bishop of Geneva, he did not retire into an administrative mold. When he was home he practiced an open door policy. When he was out on pastoral mission, which was most often the case, he was a thoroughgoing "populist," reaching out eagerly to all people and relentlessly inviting them to come to him. Capturing this attitude he said, "We bishops must be like those large public drinking fountains, where all have the right to come for water, and where not only men, but beasts and serpents drink."

His thirty-year ministry as priest and bishop in the Lake Geneva area proved to be successful in both the short and long run, for he broke the Calvinist ascendancy and recovered that area for the Church. As he described it, "When we arrived, there were not more than fifteen Catholics left in the Chablis, and now there are not more than fifteen Calvinists." He may have permitted himself a slight and forgivable exaggeration in that statement, but the substantial truth of it cannot be denied. What is left unsaid here is the fact that the religious stabilization of that territory brought an end to the cycle of religious wars and thus terminated the activity of men who would politicize religion for their own ends.

In 1604, while preaching a Lenten retreat in Dijon, he met the recently widowed Jane de Chantal. He became her spiritual adviser, and with her, became a co-founder of the Order of the Visitation.

In 1622 Francis agreed to take a physically demanding journey with the Duke of Savoy to meet the French King for the purpose of gaining some concessions. The exertions of the trip took their toll and Francis was forced to stop at the Visitation convent at Lyons, where he died from a cerebral hemorrhage.

Alexander VII canonized him on April 19, 1665.

Reflection

For a modern Church finding itself in the midst of a communications revolution, Francis de Sales looms as a friendly and encouraging figure. He was wise enough to take advantage of the comparatively new print medium of his time and put it at the service of evangelization. He understood the dynamics of his culture and was perceptive enough to see how Christ might be communicated in a fresh new way. Never abandoning personal contact, he enthusiastically embraced a novel method of communicating with astonishing success. He proved that a man of prayer could equally be a person of pragmatic programming. Francis stands as an inspiration to a Church groping for ways to make the communications revolution a means for sharing Christ's love. Francis' career should convince the Church it can be done.

Jane de Chantal

(1562–1641)

From Baroness To Mother Superior

"I cannot conclude this letter, my true and good father, without telling you that it seems to me you have not been strict enough with my daughter. But this is the way with fathers, to spoil their daughters. I know you will reply that mothers spoil their sons as well."*

Jane de Chantal, Letter to Francis de Sales

The wedding of Jane Fremyot and Christophe de Chantal reflected all the solidity of old money and the promise of secure and happy years ahead. Jane's father was the president of the parliament at Dijon and her brother was to be the archbishop of Bourges in a few years. Her new husband took her to live in a castle. Jane and Christophe were very much in love with one another, begetting six children in the first seven years of their marriage. Two of the children died at birth.

Then Jane's life fell apart. Her husband was killed in a hunting accident, a tragedy that plunged her into

---

*Francis took a fatherly interest in Francoise de Chantal, looking out for her prior to her marriage.

prolonged grief and depression. Her seventy-five-year-old father-in-law began to play the tyrant by forcing her, under threat of disinheritance, to come and live with him. The domineering old man made life miserable for an already unhappy widow. Jane de Chantal decided to seek counseling and put herself in the hands of a local spiritual director, who turned out to be a disaster. It was just her bad luck to be counseled by a man whose insight into her needs was wholly inadequate. He arbitrarily imposed on her all kinds of excessive austerities and possessively insisted that she seek out him alone for advice. He forbade her to disclose her heart to anyone else.

In retrospect, it is astonishing that Jane held onto her sanity, given the tragedy she had to absorb, the feeling of being trapped by her father-in-law and the crazed spiritual director to whom she had committed herself. Still, she had inner reserves of strength upon which she could rely, her native good sense, the values she received from her father (her mother died shortly after Jane's birth), and the years of love she had known with Christophe. She also had her children to think about.

After seven years of this, relief and hope came to her in the Lent of 1604. Her father had asked her to get away from it all by spending Lent at their family home in Dijon, where her archbishop brother would be staying for the season. It so happened that the bishop of Geneva, Francis de Sales, had agreed to give the Lenten sermons in Dijon that year, having accepted the invitation with the added purpose of settling a dispute between his diocese and that of her brother's.

Jane's listening to the sermons of de Sales was just the tonic she needed and her leisurely conversations with him during those long days of Lent proved to be the liberating experience for which she had searched so many years. Francis began restoring her self-confidence which had slowly eroded. He presented to her a spiritual process based on love, so much in contrast to the fear and guilt to which she had been exposed. He initiated in her a change in attitude that gave her a positive outlook on life and a reason for living and hoping once again.

One of the more touching results of her lenten conversion was the dawning realization that she should seek a personal reconciliation with the man who had been the unwitting cause of her husband's death. Spiritually and mentally she had forgiven him, but she never had the emotional courage to meet him or even look at him. Francis supported her in this resolve, "It is not necessary that you should fix a day for this. But if he comes, I want you, with all your heart, to be gentle, gracious and forgiving. I know your heart will not keep quiet and the blood will boil in your veins. But what does that matter? I want you to show love." Jane proceeded with the reconciliation and eighteen months later became a godmother to his new baby son.

It was clear to her now that she must break with her former spiritual director and ask Francis to be her counselor. Francis advised her to take time with this decision, though he agreed to keep in touch with her by mail. Within the year Jane disengaged herself from her old counselor and turned to Francis for direction.

As the years went by, Francis and Jane began a series of discussions about the possibility of founding a religious order of women who would combine the contemplative life with an active ministry. The rural poor were crowding into the cities and needed people to care for them and help them adapt to urban living. Traveling as much as he did, Francis was well aware of the need. In Italy the Sisters of Angela Merici, the Ursulines, were making a break with the cloistered forms of religious life for women. Francis envisioned something of that for Savoy and Dijon.

At the same time Francis saw that Jane could not involve herself in this until her family was raised and settled. Thus the planning and preparation for this new venture was extended for six years. It finally took shape on the feast of St. Norbert (a man who himself had initiated a combination of contemplative life and active ministry) June 6, 1610. Jane and two companions, at a Eucharistic celebration in the bishop's chapel, received a Rule from Francis de Sales and made a promise to God that they would begin a community life of prayer and good works. They opened their first convent at a place called Gallery House, Annecy. One year later they professed their formal vows as consecrated religious.

Their official title was the Visitation of Holy Mary. Here was an image that captured both the contemplative and human concern elements. Mary had illustrated a family concern by taking three months off to spend with her cousin Elizabeth and assist her in the final days of her pregnancy and the birth of her child. At the same time those were quiet days of contemplating the divinely wrought and mysterious conceptions of John the Baptist and Jesus. Francis and Jane concurred that this should be the direction of the new Order. Jane herself had always been drawn to mystical prayer as well as to good works for the deprived, so this development was a logical evolution in her life.

Things went well for three years until the order ran into difficulties with Cardinal Marquemont, of Lyons, where they planned to open their second convent. The bishop simply would not accept the idea of non-cloistered nuns. The idea was too new for him and he was of the conviction that the people would not put up with it. Understandably, this was a painful setback for the community and would mean a radical change in their original purpose and ideals. Jane prevailed upon Francis to seek help in Rome. Francis wrote a series of letters to Cardinal Bellarmine and received positive support for the original concept. Believing this should be sufficient, he began negotiations with Cardinal Marquemont with hopes of changing his mind. But the cardinal had made up his mind and would not tolerate non-cloistered nuns in his diocese.

Francis and Jane capitulated and transformed the Visitation Nuns into a cloistered order devoted to contemplation. It is not clear why they did not simply continue with the original ideal in Francis' own diocese of Geneva and begin their expansion there. Possibly the cardinal convinced them that this was an unworkable idea. After all they were already several years in existence. They had not grown much and they were not attracting large numbers of vocations and the latest candidates were four widows—certainly not a promising future.

Whatever might be their real reasons for following the cardinal's advice, they did submit regardless of their disappointment. Francis and Jane were primarily persuaded of the need for a religious order of women in their part of France where convent life had been devastated by the Reformation and the ensuing religious wars. While they envisioned a non-cloistered form of such life, with active ministry as a component of the sisters' lives, they both valued contemplation and agreed that contemplative convents (though cloistered) would be an important asset to the area.

As things turned out the cardinal proved correct. The Visitation Nuns began an extraordinary growth, numbering over eighty convents by the time of Jane's death, twenty-eight years after their discussions with Marquemont. And they remain a vigorous form of cloistered, contemplative living to this day, having added, as the years went on, an active ministry in education, opening the first Catholic school for girls at

Georgetown in the American colonies. The Georgetown Visitation convent and school for girls still flourishes today.

Saints are people who know how to swallow hard and get on with the business of living. Jane's life now became a flurry of action as she oversaw the establishing of the numerous convents of the order. Her collected letters reveal a woman who is compassionate, sensible and insightful. She coaxes the superior at Annecy out of depression, "You take too much to heart the inevitable happenings of life and so you worry yourself into exhaustion and depression. You must liberate yourself and not take so much to heart your lapses. Do you expect to be impeccable in this life?"

Jane was also a firm corrector of abuses. To a sister at Moulins she writes, "I cannot keep silent about your scandalous behavior. Would that my blood, dearest daughter, could cleanse the wounds of your soul and those you inflict on the house. Your callousness and self-indulgence have thrown you into this entanglement and I can see we have been too gentle with you. I pray that my grief and regret may touch your heart to change."

When Bishop Miron of Lyons wanted to force his own spiritual director on the nuns there, in contradiction to the Visitation Rule that permitted the nuns to choose their own, Jane wrote a forceful letter to the convent to resist such an imposition. She also instructed them to lock up the convent correspondence and not permit any intrusion on their privacy.

In other words Jane was involved in the typical warp and woof of the human elements that crop up in any institution, be it a convent or a business. Having managed a castle for her husband and a great house for her father-in-law, she was not blind to the ways of life. Nor did this negatively affect her growth in prayer and love.

On the day before she died, December 12, 1641, she wrote, "Dear Sisters, maintain complete simplicity of heart, poverty of life and the love that says and does to all your sisters what you would want them to say or do to you. This is all I can say to you, almost with my last breath. With all my heart I remain your sister in the Lord."

Clement XIII canonized Jane de Chantal, July 16, 1767.

Reflection

In a bewildering sort of way, Jane de Chantal is a saint who succeeded in combining some normally contradictory forms of life: wife, mother, founder of an innovative order of nuns, re-founder of that same order as a contemplative cloister. Her long life was full of sorrows and joys, but clearly joy was triumphant in the end. Like so many saints her spiritual reserves served as the source for a phenomenally energetic life and a lively imagination. Her Christian vitality should inspire those for whom it is in short supply today.

Vincent de Paul

(1580–1660)

A Dynamo of Charity

"Affective love is a flow of the person who loves into the beloved. Effective love consists in doing those things commanded or desired by the person one loves. It is this kind of love I speak."

Vincent de Paul, Lecture

The passenger liner from Marseilles to Narbonne was making good times over the comparatively peaceful Mediterranean waters. Suddenly the captain sighted the much feared Barbary pirates and tried to make a run for safety. But it was too late, for the swift pirate ships caught his boat, attacked and boarded it, wounding and killing many of the crew and passengers, among whom was the newly ordained Vincent de Paul returning from Toulouse where he had collected an inheritance.

They took Vincent to Tunis and sold him as a slave to an alchemist. Vincent later described the process of the sale, "They made us open our mouths to see our teeth. They were feeling our sides, examining our wounds, making us walk, trot and run, making us carry weights and fight so as to gauge our strength." After some time with the alchemist, Vincent was sold to an ex-priest and apostate who lived on a plantation with his three wives.

Though Vincent at this time, by his own admission, was not a man of deep faith, he was a true believer and a newly graduated bachelor in theology. Somehow he touched the conscience of his master, converted him back to the Church with the result that Vincent gained his freedom and the two of them sailed for France. (It is not clear what happened to the three wives.)

Vincent de Paul had been born on a small farm in Landes. He did not like being on a farm and decided that ordination to the priesthood would be his ticket to freedom. He was lucky to find a patron, De Comet, the magistrate of the county who took a liking to Vincent and agreed to pay for his clerical education. Vincent's native shrewdness and lack of funds made him somewhat of an opportunist during his youth. He acquired the art of ingratiating himself with others, such as De Comet, to advance his own career. It was probably just such a skill that won him the inheritance from the widow of Toulouse, the voyage from which occasioned his fateful capture and enslavement in Tunis.

The man who would become the greatest champion of the poor was dedicating his youthful career as a priest to becoming a rich and secure clergyman. The slavery setback did not chasten his conscience, for no sooner was he back in France than he made for Avignon with his friend, intending to meet the Pope's Legate for the ostensible purpose of having his friend restored to priesthood—and to see what might be in this for himself. Most successful opportunists are persons of considerable charm, and Vincent was apparently no exception.

The Legate was beguiled by Vincent's appealing ways and his stories of pirates, alchemists and African planters. He took Vincent under his wing and brought him to Rome, where the young priest, eager as ever to advance himself, easily made important contacts and began to dream of high advancement in the Church. After eighteen months in Rome, he judged that the next step had to be Paris. Armed with letters of introduction from a host of important people, he arrived in Paris and began making contacts. In quick time he secured an appointment as chaplain to the Queen of Navarre, to which income he added a yearly grant from St. Leonard's Cistercian abbey. He was achieving the prosperity and prominence he had sought for so long.

What he had not suspected is that he would meet people in high places who would change his whole self-aggrandizing attitude. In the salon of Queen Margaret he came in touch with Cardinal Berulle, founder of the French Oratory and destined to be known as the reformer of the clergy of France. Vincent was accustomed to bringing others under his spell, but now met his match in Berulle who played the first role of several who would bring Vincent to his moment of truth and honesty. Berulle awakened a dormant spiritual and moral awareness in Vincent that drew him away from his opportunism and planted in him a sense of a genuine Christian calling.

This was accentuated by a year's absence from the glittering reception rooms of Paris, for, unaccountably, Vincent accepted a post as pastor in the Appalachia-like farming area of Chatillons. He found that his natural talent for accommodation and charm was now effectively brought to bear upon these forgotten people. When he discovered that whole pockets of them were on the verge of starvation and utter destitution, he was moved immediately to do something about it. Not given to preaching much or theorizing about poverty, he vigorously organized disciplined teams of charity activists who provided a regular service of food, clothing and hope for these unfortunates. These teams developed into the "Confraternity of the Ladies of Charity."

Within the year he was summoned back to Paris to serve as a kind of chief campus minister for the prominent Gondi family. They wanted him to repeat his miracle of religious renewal and charitable efforts for the hundreds of peasants who lived on their thousands of country acres. Just as the Gondi's were reaching into the reserves of Vincent to bring forth his possibilities in the area of charity, Francis de Sales happened to be in Paris. Vincent's meeting with Francis seems to have finally stabilized and deepened his conversion from a superficial clerical courtier to a genuine generous-hearted Christian. Not only was Vincent totally captivated by the irresistible Francis, he even found himself agreeing to be the ecclesiastical superior of the Visitation convents in Paris as well as the new spiritual director of Jane de Chantal. (Francis de Sales died that year, 1622.)

For the next thirty-eight years Vincent kept a schedule that would destroy many a modern executive. With six other priests he formed a mission team that moved out into the villages of the Gondi estates, holding what we could very well call religious revival meetings, or "missions" that were meant to bring the people back to the faith. At the same time, they initiated the charity teams which Vincent had invented at Chatillons.

Vincent began to realize that the devastating state of religion among the country people was due to the ignorance and spiritual impoverishment of the clergy. To meet this problem, Vincent instituted the Tuesday Conferences for the zealous priests of Paris and then devised a ten day retreat for seminarians preparing for the priesthood. This latter retreat model was used widely thereafter and considered to be a profound conversion experience for many seminarians. Vincent went even further, by establishing a seminary according to the new norms of the Council of Trent as well as his own ideas of what a ministry-minded priest ought to be. The mission team that he had created for evangelizing the countryside became the nucleus of a religious order, the Congregation of the Mission, or the Vincentians as they are known in the United States. These men helped staff Vincent's new seminary concept, and in the centuries to follow it became common for bishops to ask this order to staff their seminaries.

In the midst of all this activity Vincent's group was offered the vacated leper's hospital, St. Lazare, along with its lands for his use. He accepted it and made it the central house of his order as well as a "Noah's Ark" for every kind of charitable undertaking.

Barely missing a beat while organizing St. Lazare, Vincent began creating "Little Households," basically nursing homes for senior citizens, where elderly husbands and wives might spend their final days. He also sent ten of his priests to serve as chaplains in the army, while thinking about how he was going to organize effective relief services for Lorraine which had been devastated by the wars of religion.

While these many projects competed for his attention, the Queen of France invited him to be a member of the "Council of Conscience," a royal effort to put some morals into the government. One would not think that should be a problem, given the fact that a Cardinal of the Church, Mazarin, was the prime minister, but recalling that Mazarin's interests were totally political, one may—as the record shows—infer that gospel values were not exactly his highest priority. Vincent served on this Council until such time as it became apparent that he would never get anywhere so long as Mazarin was in charge.

The Gondi family, which had done so much to help Vincent get into the rural mission work, was also connected with the administration of the royal navy and its galley slaves. They made Vincent the chaplain for the slaves, a job that appealed to him, given his own experience with slavery as a young man. He did what he could to minimize the brutality associated with their state and badgered his rich friends with begging notes, thus collecting large sums of money to ransom the slaves and obtain their freedom. As in the case of Peter Claver, he was not able to abolish the institution of slavery, but he did as much as he was able.

One of his top assistants on the charity teams was Louise de Marillac. Recalling Francis de Sales' frustration with the change in his concept for a religious order of women, Vincent decided to avoid some of de Sales' problems by forming a group of women for the purpose of charitable work, but without any of the trappings of a religious order, thus being outside the traditional Church laws on the matter. They would be called the "Sisters of Charity, whose convent would be the sick room, whose chapel was the parish church, whose cloister would be the city streets." Vincent composed their rule, gave them conferences and governed them as superior general. They would become a hugely successful order, numerous, inspiring and effective.

His concept of lay involvement in works of charity was taken up later by Frederick Ozanam, whose St. Vincent de Paul Societies still remain a widespread and important witness to this mission.

It must be remembered that Vincent did all this without the benefit of telephone, automobile or plane, or any other of the conveniences so common now. How in the world he still found time to write over three thousand letters remains a mystery. Nor does he seem to have been a mystic, at least not in the traditional sense. Definitely he was a man of prayer and totally committed to Christ, that much we can affirm without question. His motivation arose from the purest of love for Christ and for people.

This energetic man, so full of love because he had given so much, died in Paris, September 27, 1660. He was canonized in 1737.

Reflection

Vincent was a doer in an age when action-oriented
religion was becoming an accepted part of spirituality.
His capacity for work is astonishing by any standards
and his ability to organize efforts for charitable
purposes can hardly be equalled. We puzzle today over
unresponsive bureaucracies. Perhaps we need the kind
of get-action man that Vincent was. The Church's poor
today cry out for social change. Were he alive now, it
is quite possible that is exactly where Vincent would
be. Surely the poor—and all of us—would be the better
for it.

Louise de Marillac

(1591–1660)

A Radical Thinker and Activist

"I die having the highest esteem for our vocation.
Were I to live for a hundred years, I would not ask
anything else of you but to remain faithful to it."
Louise de Marillac, Last Words

Seventeenth-century Paris possessed many of the
characteristics of the nineteenth-century London, so
well described in the novels of Charles Dickens or the
paintings of Hogarth, a city of grinding poverty offset
by the majesty of Notre Dame and the palaces and
mansions of the rich. "Oliver Twists," or foundlings,
were to be seen by the thousands in a so-called
receiving center, known as La Couche, where
professional beggars collected them for training as
thieves, even mutilating them to arouse pity if they
were to be used as motivators for the begging process.
The city swarmed with beggars, cripples, syphilitic
persons and criminals of every sort. The overcrowded
jails and poorhouses and debtors prisons were a
reminder that no such idea as prison reform had yet
touched the social conscience of the people. Paris had
its own versions of "Gin Lane," countless alleys and
narrow streets filled with the poor drugged by cheap
wine.

It was into these pitiful worlds that the refined thirty-six-year-old widow, Louise de Marillac, led her volunteer "Ladies of Charity," doing what they could to relieve the misery. Inspired by Vincent de Paul and committed to his vision of social concern, Louise became his chief executive in overseeing these charity teams both in Paris and in the provinces. During her five-year supervision of this project, she became the soul of the movement.

A tough-minded realist, Louise realized that the movement suffered some major drawbacks. The major problem was that of all volunteer organizations, the dependability, dedication and long-term commitment of the volunteers. The *ad hoc* quality of a volunteer group meant that attempts to help the poor would be intermittent, short-term, and woefully insufficient if there would be any hope of making significant headway in containing the advance of poverty and providing a roadway of hope for the poor.

Another stumbling block was the refined sensibility of the ladies. They were simply too well bred and accustomed to cleanliness and gentleness to be able to get in there and put up with the smells and dirt, let along to be physically fit to do the scrubbing, lifting, pulling, pushing, painting and washing that would be needed to provide a fresh environment for the sick, the old and the children. Pampered by servants all of their lives, they were in no mood very often, nor prepared to cope with the emotional and physical demands that charity work required.

Slowly Louise came to the conclusion that another kind of woman would be needed for this enterprise. Why not recruit strong country girls, accustomed to hard work to serve as special helpers in the charity teams? She managed to bring aboard a few of these good village girls to see how they would work out. She found exactly what she was looking for, hard working, willing and able women who took to the social service efforts with rough-hewn dedication and humming efficiency. This was the beginning of the "Daughters of Charity."

It took Louise a while to find a way to make the best use of these redoubtable new helpers. At first she dispersed small groups of them among the other charity teams, but the ladies in the other groups did not quite know how to handle these country women, serving with them as equals, and not as maids. So Louise assembled them at her own home which was now transformed into a kind of convent, though the term would not be used for reasons that will be noted in a moment. This happened in November, 1633, a date that may serve as the founding of the Daughters of Charity.

Vincent assisted them in composing a rule of life and devised the striking motto, "Leave God for God." They should pray indeed, but be ready to leave prayer to go and serve the poor who are the representatives of God, since they would find Christ in the poor. With their hearts they were to share their love (affective love), and with their service they were to share their energies (effective love).

Louise was faced with an organizational problem that concerned the status of her women in the eyes of the Church and society. She could take some guidance from the Ursulines of Angela Merici, whose convents were centers of education for women, and she could ponder the frustrations of Jane de Chantal who was forced to regroup her women back in cloisters so soon after the founding of the Visitation nuns. Louise wanted her women to work the streets and not be confined either to convents or cloisters.

Together with Vincent de Paul, Louise devised an ingenious compromise that by-passed the traditional forms of nuns' lives and the prevailing restrictions in Church law.

She decided first of all there was no need to call themselves a religious order. They would simply be a "Company" or association of women committed to social service. They would not live in a building called a convent or monastery, but merely a "house." The superior would not be an abbess, prioress or mother general; she would be a sister servant of her companions. They took no vows in the formal sense of the word, professing instead a kind of "gentlewoman's agreement" to be poor, chaste, obedient and service oriented. During Louise's lifetime they did evolve somewhat toward vows, but these were always to be made privately and could only be taken for one year. This arrangement was an artifice that worked very well, enabling Vincent de Paul to argue persuasively with the authorities for their existence and right to work in such a manner.

Just as the education of women was wrested from the exclusive rights of the cloisters by Angela Merici, so now the vocation to social service was expanded from the exclusive domains of clerics and rich women by Louise and her Daughters of Charity, thus liberated to work the streets, establish hospitals, orphanages, nursing homes and other similar institutions.

What were the Daughters to wear? Louise decided that the typical clothing of a peasant woman would serve very well as a uniform, so they wore a gray dress and cloak, and wrapped their heads with a simple white scarf. This is why they were called "Gray Sisters" up to the time of the French Revolution. Years later when Napoleon was asked to comment on how wonderful were the benefits of philanthropy in the Age of Enlightenment, he answered, "All that is good and well, gentlemen, but give us a Gray Sister anytime." Only after the Revolution did they begin wearing a blue dress and the picturesque headgear that reminded some of sails.

Louise and her Daughters of Charity now embarked on a series of projects for which a highly motivated, well organized group of persons were well suited. For one thing, the hospitals of the time were wretched places, overcrowded, dirty and poorly administered. The Daughters took over the deplorable Hotel-Dieu, a rat hole of a hospital, and transformed it into a model hospital for Paris and the world. Efficiency, orderliness and watchfulness became key components in their approach.

The Daughters rose at four in the morning and spent two hours in prayer followed by what was then the "continental breakfast" of bread and wine. Then they scrubbed their hands with vinegar and swarmed into the wards to greet the patients, make beds, sweep floors and administer medicines. They brought the patients breakfast at seven and spent the remainder of the morning visiting with the patients, comforting them, teaching them the basics of faith, and motivating them to a positive attitude based on religious faith. They would understand very well the modern approach of wholistic medicine that deals with attitudes, as well as curing symptoms, in treating the sick, and would resonate approvingly with Norman Cousins' defense of this in his *Anatomy of an Illness.*

At two o'clock they served the patients cooked apples and pears, along with preserves and sugared toast. At four they administered the typical medical panaceas of the day, bleedings and purgations, and changed the linens of the insane, paralyzed and bedridden patients. After the evening meal, they urged the patients to go to sleep as well as they could, and then retired for their own examination of conscience, the recitation of the Litany of the Blessed Virgin and some meditation. They blessed the patients with holy water and then went to bed.

The sick were never left alone, for some of the Daughters would stay with them while the community was at prayer, and some would take turns sitting with them through the night. Hence the Daughters were always ready for emergencies, as well as for the surgeries for which no time slot could necessarily be scheduled. They created a total approach to hospital care, that included cleanliness, prayer, affection, nutrition, friendliness and a positive attitude.

This extended description of what they were able to do for hospital reform is an example of how they were to expand their talents to orphanages, nursing homes, field clinics in war, beggars' hostels and any other kind of social service their inventive and dedicated spirits could devise. For twenty-seven years, Louise and her attentive spiritual counselor, Vincent, oversaw the careful growth and expansion of these multiple ministries all over Europe and eventually into mission countries.

Amazingly, though Louise was a woman of frail health, she somehow found the inner power, from Christ as she testifies, to supervise personally and strictly the implementation of her ideals. She loved the poor with all her heart, thus flowing with affective love. She served them with every ounce of energy, determined to give them effective love. She died with the perfectly warranted confidence that her dream would endure. History verifies her trust, for today the Daughters of Charity survive as effectively and affectively loving as ever—and one of the largest "Company" of such women in the world.

The Church canonized Louise de Marillac in 1934.

Reflection

We hear a great deal today about being radical in one's approach. We have a tendency to believe we are the first to be so daring. One of the values of reading history is to discover that radical thinking has occurred many times before as illustrated in the dramatic and daring life of Louise de Marillac. The challenge before us is this: Are we yet radical or daring enough, given the needs of today's poor?

John Baptist de la Salle

(1651–1719)

Avant-Garde Educator

"It is not enough to prevent those under your care from doing wrong. You must also persuade them to perform as many good works as possible."

La Salle, Advice to Educators

Seventeenth-century France was the last place one might expect to find the emergence of an avant-garde educator. The royal absolutism of the "Sun King," Louis XIV, and the ecclesiastical conservatism of the Cardinals who served as his Prime Ministers yielded little or no room for innovators. Education was for the rich only, be they the ruling aristocrats or the newly rising middle class of merchants. State supported schools for the poor, who constituted the largest part of the population, were unknown. If anyone paid any attention to the education of the poor, it was the local parish priest, an occasional good-hearted rich woman, or one of the new religious orders experimenting with the idea. The best one could say about the education of the poor was that it was chaotic, mismanaged, dismally staffed by wretched schoolmasters and lacking any long-range value for the students, or the country for that matter.

The unlikely candidate for changing all this was John Baptist de la Salle, a rich and cultivated French gentleman, accustomed to the mannered conversations of the *salon* and cushioned from the noise and dirt of the poor by money, power and prestige. An ordained priest, he served as a Cathedral Canon at Rheims where he enjoyed the lesiurely life of a scholar, little affected by the small interruptions of Cathedral duties. (The "Higher Clergy" were not expected to bother with pastoral obligations. That was for what we would call the "blue collar" priests.)

La Salle was a good man, but he did not instinctively have a social conscience nor much interest in justice issues. In fact he did not like the poor and was repelled by their smells and coarse behavior. He did however believe in practicing what he preached and he possessed a relentless ability to be practical. When he discovered his calling to be an educator of poor children, he approached the problem, not with the passion of a theorist afire with justice ideals, but simply with his awesome pragmatism, "There's a job to do. Let's get at it."

The France of his day was experiencing a ferment of interest in the education of the poor. It was an idealistic schoolmaster named Ryel who caused La Salle to become interested in the question. Ryel was an enthusiast, a visionary, who had little administrative talent. He was an idea man, but not an implementer. He would start a school, but had no patience with seeing to its daily continuance. He was a thinker more than a doer. In La Salle he found the man who was the doer more than the thinker. La Salle was intrigued by Ryel's new school for the poor in Rheims, financed by a local rich lady.

La Salle rented a home for the five schoolmasters, probably as a simple act of good will for the new project, but not with any idea of deeper involvement. He was not personally impressed with the quality of the teachers and would agree with the prevailing low opinion of them as expressed by Demia of Lyons. "The greater number of teachers did not only not know how to read and write well, but were also ignorant of the principles of religion." The Bishop of Touls was not pleased either when he reported, "They are gamblers, drunkards, libertines, ignorant and brutal. They pass their days in taverns, playing cards and play the fiddle at the haunts of pleasure."

Ill paid, poorly trained and uncertain of their future, these teachers could hardly be expected to be self-assured professionals. La Salle hated to see inefficient behavior, and, despite his dislike of these people, he could not resist the urge to get in there and put some order and discipline into their lives. He brought the teachers into his own home and began to upgrade their personal behavior and professional stance. Slowly it began to dawn on him that God was calling him to devote his life to the training of teachers and the education of poor children. In that elegant home of the sensitive Cathedral Canon, La Salle, the idea of the Order of the Brothers of the Christian Schools was born.

It soon became evident to La Salle that his credibility with the teachers depended upon his willingness to share in their own financial vulnerability. Until he shared in the same insecurity about the future that they endured, he would not have the moral impact on them he desired. Practicing what he preached, he divested himself of all his money and possessions and resigned his salaried post as a Cathedral Canon. Unencumbered by wealth or position, La Salle devoted the rest of his life and energies to his new calling.

There was no doubt in his mind that faith, prayer, order and discipline should constitute the core of his training program for the schoolmasters. He was determined to awaken in them a strong sense of self-respect and infuse them with a tenacious belief in the excellence of their calling as teachers. By rooting them in a deeply religious atmosphere he was convinced he would achieve just such goals. Gradually the concept of forming them into a religious Order of Brothers took shape. Over the years, and after numerous discussions, the principal outlines of the new Order emerged. He diverted their attention from the style of the old monastic Orders and the new Jesuit approaches. For one thing, they were mainly clergy models and secondly they were not involved in the education of the urban poor. He reminded them of their calling as Brothers whose ministerial goal was precise and different. Lest they drift over to becoming clergy, he trained a Brother to become the superior of the Order and eventually resigned his post. The Brothers were founded by a priest, but learned how to govern themselves as Brothers within the unique charism of the vocation of Brothers.

La Salle was equally interested in creating free and first-class education for the poor. He realized that the poor needed career opportunities if they were to use their education for upward mobility. Hence he decided the classes should be taught in French instead of the customary Latin. Let the rich learn in Latin which will not hold them back since they already have contacts in the world to make their way. The poor need immediate training in French, both to read and write fluently for purposes of career advancement. La Salle was not against the cultural advantages of Latin, but did not believe that one needed to study Latin in order to learn how to write and argued that training in one's own native language is the best way to begin. This is not an innovative thought for us, but it was a revolutionary idea in seventeenth-century France. His concept worked so well that the writing masters in other schools were losing their students to the La Salle schools, causing, as one might predict, some uproars and political intimidation of the new schools.

A second innovation was La Salle's introduction of "Simultaneous Instruction," that is, teaching the whole class the same subject at the same time, instead of individualized instruction for each student. Again this is something taken for granted by our own age, but then it was unheard of. Today we look for some individualized treatment in a class situation, but in La Salle's day attending only to individuals meant havoc for the teacher. La Salle saw that one of the worst problems in the classrooms of his time, especially among the poor in primary schools, was disorder, which the schoolmasters countered with cruelty to the children. La Salle trained his teachers to be disciplinarians by being well-prepared, by keeping the students occupied, and by maintaining a religious and civil environment in the school.

La Salle was fond of writing minute, practical instructions for every aspect of classroom life. For example on discipline, he advises: (1) Pupils should never be slapped or kicked. (2) It is unworthy of the dignity of the teacher to pull the children's noses, ears or hair. (3) Never make a child cry. (4) Never use insulting words to the children. (5) No punishment must be harmful to him who receives it. La Salle would not have made such rules if he had not known of such abuses.

La Salle put enormous emphasis on the religious quality of the school. He seemed to operate from the axiom: "The more genuinely religious a school is, the more academically successful it will be." He proved to be right. He prescribed strong doses of religion and religious practices for the daily schedule. Again the maxim writer, La Salle takes little for granted: (1) Teach catechism daily for half an hour. (2) Teach them the maxims of the Gospels and the prayers of the Church and show them how to apply these to their lives. The school day was interspersed with prayers.

Participation in liturgies, both on Sunday and at other times, was taken for granted. At the same time he demanded high academic performance from both teachers and students alike.

The key to his whole program was intense and constant training of the teachers both as religious brothers and professional instructors. It was his belief that their self-worth and professional image arose from being men striving for holiness and pedagogical competence. A persistent observer of teachers' behavior, he listed what he wanted to draw them away from: "(1) Fickleness; (2) Itching to talk; (3) Harshness; (4) Partiality; (5) Giddiness; (6) Petulance; (7) Time wasting;" and a host of other frailties.

One of his most innovative creations was the "Special School" in which he provided education for delinquent children—mostly from the wealthier classes. Instead of sending the boys to prisons or houses for the insane, people sent them to La Salle's special schools where they were treated humanely. At first confined to their rooms, where they were allowed to have bird cages and raise flowers in their window boxes, then gradually drawn out by the Brother counselor, they were often able to return to a wholesome life in the world. Occupational therapy shops were provided for teaching them a trade.

In summary, La Salle was an educational genius whose personal sanctity provided him with both the motivation and inner spiritual power to bring about the educational innovations he achieved. Like all innovators, La Salle faced plenty of opposition from the state, the Church, and other educators whose pet theories he was exploding and whose performance his Brothers were upstaging. But he was not a man to wallow in self-pity or spend much time in public debate. Always business-like and practical, he forged ahead, establishing his schools and training his beloved Brothers and even founding teacher training schools (called "Normal Schools") for laymen who liked his ideals but did not wish to enter religious life.

La Salle died on Good Friday, 1719. Pope Leo XIII canonized him in 1900. Pius XII declared him patron of all teachers in 1950.

Reflection

In many of today's Church-related schools there is considerable bashfulness about being consciously and specifically religious. Practices of piety have virtually disappeared and nothing new has replaced them. The academic quality is fine, but the religious awareness could use some inspiration from La Salle's forthright idea that the more religious a school is the more academic it can be. He saw no contradiction in his own day. He would argue there should not be any in ours either.

Therese of Lisieux

(1873–1897)

The Little Woman Was a Giant

"After my death I shall let fall a shower of roses . . .
I shall come back to earth and teach others to love
Love."

Therese of Lisieux, Autobiography

What do you say about a twenty-four-year-old nun
who died of tuberculosis? In the case of Therese of
Lisieux, plenty. This was not the opinion of her
Carmelite sisters who paused outside her sickroom and
wondered, as one of them put it, "Therese will die
soon. What will the Prioress be able to write for her
obituary? 'She entered our convent, lived and died.
There really is no more to say.' "

Yet within a few months of her death a storm of
interest and affection for Therese began that a Vatican
Cardinal declared, "We must hasten to canonize
Therese, otherwise we shall be anticipated by the voice
of the people." The Vatican indeed broke its traditional
rule of not starting a canonization process until fifty
years after a person's death, by naming Therese a
saint in 1925. (Had Therese been alive, she would have
only been 52.)

Her obituary had a lot to do with this, because it
was more than a death notice. It happened to be a
journal in which Therese had recorded some childhood

memories, girlhood experiences and a series of practical lessons about convent living. Entitled *The Story of a Soul,* the book had been written for her older sisters, also Carmelites, and sent out to the convents as a Memorial book. The book had an extraordinary impact upon its readers and the demand for it was overwhelming. By 1932 over 800,000 copies of the book were in circulation, plus two and a half million copies of an abridged version in the original language alone. At the time of her canonization the book had been translated into thirty-five languages. And these figures have enormously increased since then.

What accounted for this unforeseen interest in *The Story of a Soul?* At first it was due to the astonishing fulfillment of a promise Therese made in her book, "After my death, I will let fall a shower of roses." People took her at her word and sought miracles and spiritual favors through her intercession, so that by 1925 the Carmel at Lisieux documented answers to such prayers in volumes of three thousand pages, reporting (with medical affidavits) cures of cancer, ulcers, blindness, meningitis, and so forth, as well as religious conversions and just plain peace of heart. Here one finds stories of rescues, conversions, cures and liberation from prisons, plagues and floods in Chinese villages, Moslem strongholds in Algeria, cities in India, South African farms, Manchuria, New York, the Solomon Islands, Alaska and Thailand.

Beyond this reason, another line from Therese contributed to the popular affection for her, "I shall come back to earth to teach others to *love Love.*" Millions felt that love and returned it with enthusiasm, such as the Madagascar orphans and Japanese lepers who went without rice to make a donation to build her basilica in Lisieux, or the African priests in the Congo who placed themselves under her protection, or the Canadian city that sent a thousand pilgrims to celebrate an anniversary of her canonization. Even the

Protestants were touched, such as the Anglicans at Walsingham who reverently exhibited a relic (piece of her blanket). And in Iran, a Shiite Moslem, whose faith is exceptionally hostile to images, kept a picture publicly posted of the Therese who brought him a cure, stating, "Neither Mohammed nor the prophets outweigh this lovely saint."

Which brings us to the third and clearly most important reason for Therese's exceptional influence, her life. The story line is comparatively uneventful. Born in Alencon, France, the youngest of nine children, Therese Martin, daughter of Louis Martin, a watchmaker and his wife Zelie Guerin, was raised in Lisieux by her elder sisters and an aunt after the death of her mother when Theresa was five. Outwardly her childhood was marked by the usual comforts and annoyances of a cozy, middle-class family of the nineteenth century.

The father leaned to the devout side and encouraged a sense of piety in his family, with the result that his two oldest daughters entered the Carmelite convent at Lisieux. Early on Therese seems to have had a precocious interest in spiritual matters. It was also clear that she possessed unusual powers of concentration, so that beneath the flowery femininity and language of endearment that was the fashion of the times, there resided in the awareness of Therese a granite-hard resolve and single-minded determination to pursue an inner attraction to God. With the utmost candor she could say, "I have never refused the good God anything" and mean it. Not that she was immune to moods and small expected tantrums as in any growing young girl, but that after the storm she resolutely returned to her stated goal of union with Love.

At the age of fourteen she began making noises about joining her sisters at the Lisieux Carmel. It did not seem to matter to her that she was too young, or that her doting father would miss her, or that prudence and common-sense experience would demand a delay. Moreover, some worried that having three nuns from the same family in a small Carmel, limited to twenty members, would be just a bit too much. Therese campaigned vigorously to achieve her goal. First, she brought her father around to her point of view. Then she found an unexpected ally in the Prioress, Marie de Gonzague, who, unaccountably, decided to back Therese's wish. But Therese found the usual opposition one might reasonably expect from her pastor and the bishop who simply argued she was too young.

About this time her father took her and one older sister on a pilgrimage to Rome, a month-long trip that was largely a sight-seeing holiday for the prosperous Catholics on the tour. Marie de Gonzague advised her to ask the Pope himself for permission, and this she was resolved to do. Her account of the trip reveals her single-mindedness, because she has relatively little to say about the glorious art and architecture that would normally have touched her otherwise impressionable sensitivities. Coming from a brotherless environment, Therese coped for the first time with the attention of young men, one of whom fell in love with her during the trip, as Celine testified at the canonization trial. Therese is touched but determined to be a Carmelite, while alluding to this incident, "I feel that my heart is easily caught by tenderness, and where others fall I would fall too. . . . We are no stronger than the others."

In Rome the pilgrims were presented to Leo XIII. Each pilgrim came and knelt before the Pope, kissing his foot and then his hand, while the Vicar General introduced the person. Then the Pope would say a few words, bless the pilgrim and give him or her a medal. Just before Therese's turn, the Vicar General announced that no one should speak to the Pope, but at that same instant, Celine whispered to her sister, "Speak!"

And Therese did, "Holy Father, in honor of your jubilee, let me enter Carmel at fifteen." The Vicar General interrupted her, "Your Holiness, the superiors at Carmel are going into the question." "Very well," said the Pope, "let the superiors decide." Therese clasped her hands on the Pope's knee and spoke to him as though he were her own father, "If you said yes, everyone else would be willing." Leo XIII just looked at her, and finally said, "Well . . . Well . . . You will enter if it is God's will." As they led her away, the Pope laid his hand on Therese's lips, a gesture hard to interpret in retrospect. She was deeply disappointed and compared the ruins of Pompeii to her own mood, "I longed to walk among the ruins and ponder how transient all things are."

Once home, she waited out the weeks and months for a reply, anxiously checking the mail each day. The Bishop's approval finally came on December 28, but she would have to wait until after Lent. On April 9, 1888 Therese entered the Carmel at Lisieux. She writes, "My dream was at last realized, and peace flooded my soul. . . . It has never left me these eight and a half years." At the age of fifteen she had entered a solitude to which she was totally convinced God had drawn her. The enviable concentration, with which she had been gifted, now found a worthy object, or better said, subject, for the God of love laid absolute claim to her affections, and she never wavered in her attention to the call. Her inward journey can scarcely be chartered in words and it remains a mystery, like painting the gleam of a candle in the noonday sunshine. At best we only intuit it and catch some light from her writings and the plain details of her life.

She made her novitiate, professed her vows and formally "took the veil." Her father grew ill enough to be taken to a sanitarium. Three years after her entry, a flu epidemic ravaged the convent, killing three of the nuns. It is believed Therese's own health then began to break down due to overstrain in caring for her sisters. Her father died soon after this and her sister became Prioress, at which point Celine joined her three sisters at the Carmel. In June, 1897, Therese, at the request of her sister Pauline, began writing *The Story of a Soul* and completed it just before her death, which occurred on September 30, 1897. On October 4, she was buried in the town cemetery of Lisieux.

In her autobiography she refers often to the efforts of her father and the convent sisters to spoil her and hold her back from entering strenuously into the life of Carmel. To the comfort-loving people of the period, the austerities of Carmel—the straw pallets, fasting and vigils—awakened awe. People became protective about this young girl and wanted to soften the situation. She, however, considered herself to be a woman of iron health and welcomed the thrill of the challenge, taking it on in the spirit of any young person testing his or her mettle.

To her, these were simply ways of helping her onward through the inward journey she had begun. She loved the challenges. It all became a matter of simplifying life for her. This is why she found the Gospels part of that direct and uncomplicated search for Christ's love. Ultimately, this is the secret of her appeal to so many millions. She disclosed the purest meaning of Gospel living, which is what she meant when she declared, "I will teach all people to love Love."

Reflection

Much is made of the term "little" in her life—"Little Therese, the Little Way." Actually the little woman was a giant. "Little" never meant small or sweet or limp to her. It really referred to a simplicity, a trait found in geniuses whether religious or otherwise. Her culture and religious traditions were stuffed with doo-dads as suffocating as the sofas and drawing rooms of the middle class of the day. Her "little" is more akin to the "Small is beautiful" and "Less is more" tastes of our own culture. This is the reason she has captivated the intellectuals while retaining mass appeal at the same time. With unusual clarity she made the depths of the interior prayer and selfless love as available to the mighty as to the humble. And they have both loved her and the Christ to whom she points. What more could one expect of a saint?

Bernadette
of Lourdes

(1844–1879)

Where God Kissed the Earth

"The Lady said to me: 'Go and drink at the spring, and
wash yourself in it.' "

Bernadette, The Ninth Appearance

One of the oldest and most persistent of all religious
instincts is the inner drive to make a pilgrimage. Some
may argue that this is little more than a spiritual form
of the normal human wish to take a trip. That may be,
but the evidence remains that often the motive for a
trip is a spiritual one, as observed by Mircea Eliade,
one of the ranking scholars on comparative religions.
As he points out, people are especially moved to
embark on a religious journey to a place where some
primordial experience of God has occurred, some
sacred space, where—as he describes it—"God has
kissed the earth."

People appear drawn to such places if a mystical
experience occurred there, or a martyrdom of a holy
person took place. Religious-minded Jews today
journey to the Wailing Wall, near the site of the
Temple where it is believed that Abraham, about to
sacrifice his son Isaac, had a deep experience of God
that brought about the sparing of his son. Moslems by
the millions travel to Mecca to imbibe some of the
religious spirit of Mohammed who had a profound

experience of God there by the great stone that is also associated with Abraham, the father of faith experiences.

Medieval Christian pilgrims flocked to Canterbury to be touched by the courageous spirit of the martyred Becket and perhaps obtain a desired miracle or a new lease on life. Eliade notes a common element in the search of the pilgrims, that they come to absorb the "mana" of the place, the divine power that hovers around this sacred space, a holy force that may produce miracles, conversions, renewals.

The pilgrimage spirit is alive and well among modern Catholics who journey by the countless thousands, sometimes millions, to Rome, Jerusalem and possibly the most popular place of all—Lourdes, where an estimated million pilgrims visit each year. The grotto at Lourdes, maintained to a great extent in its original simplicity, evokes the mystical associations one might expect from a revered holy space. A recessed rock formation, adjacent to the swift flow of the mountain-fed Gave River, the space itself draws one into a meditative mood. The shrine church on the hill above is sufficiently out of the way, and the busyness of the town of Lourdes is walled out.

Catholics believe that in this place, a French teenage peasant girl, Bernadette Soubirous, experienced eighteen visions of the Virgin Mary, from February 1858 to July 1859. Bernadette testified that the "Lady" asked her to encourage people to be more prayerful, to call them to self-restraint and personal discipline, to build a church by this place and to "drink from the spring." Bernadette unearthed a source of spring water nearby that has become a focal point ever since for a broad variety of healings, miracles, cures, conversions and general faith renewal of countless numbers of people. Among the most famous of those mysteriously affected by the "mana-power" of Lourdes was the Jewish author, Franz Werfel, whose book *The Song of*

Bernadette became a best seller and the basis of a film that proved to have wide popular appeal.

Aside from her eighteen-month involvement with the visions at the grotto, Bernadette's life of thirty-five years falls into two phases, each of which is characterized by normal, undramatic sequences. Before the visions she lives out fourteen years of her life as a French peasant girl, raised in a family of limited means. After the visions she spends the remainder of her eighteen years as a prayerful nun in the cloister at Nevers.

The first-born child of Francois Soubirous, an unsuccessful miller, and his wife Louise, Bernadette, and the brothers and sisters to come, endured the poverty that ensued after the failure of their mill and their consequent bankruptcy. This meant, among other things, that they would show little interest in Bernadette's education. In her growing years she served, as older sisters often did, as surrogate mother to the enlarging family. In her eleventh year she was farmed out for a while to a foster mother where she earned her keep as a shepherdess. Though a fairly robust young girl, she gradually began to have asthma attacks that progressively weakened her constitution.

Her mother had communicated to her the strong doses of piety that were common enough among the French people of the period, the difference being that Bernadette seemed to respond to this training in faith more spontaneously than most. She began to regret her lack of education because it prevented her from knowing enough catechism to gain admission to First Communion, usually celebrated then in one's twelfth year. Her foster mother made some attempts to teach her, sometimes spending as much as two hours a night, but not with much success. "The same word had to be repeated to her three or four times, and still she did not remember it," testified Jean-Marie Garros, "so that her foster mother would say to her, 'You will never learn anything.' " This remains a puzzling aspect of Bernadette's life, since she evidently liked the idea of making her First Communion, both because it was a matter of social custom and the fact she wanted communion so much.

In her fourteenth year, Bernadette insisted on going back to live in her own home, despite her father's objections about his inability to support her. But home she came and very soon became the center of a series of events that would make her name and the town of Lourdes irrevocably famous. She finally began to make some headway in the rudiments of an education and joined enthusiastically in the upkeep of the household, a shabby slum dwelling at the edge of town. The dampness of their basement rooms caused an increase of her asthma attacks.

One morning, Bernadette, with her sister and girlfriend, went off to gather some firewood. Part of their plan was to ford the icy waters of the Gave River near a grotto. They told Bernadette to stay behind because of her asthma. She waited there impatiently by the large stone recess and began to pray to pass the time. To the right of the grotto was an oval niche, bordered by the branches of a wild rose bush.

Bernadette was just about to take off her stockings and join her companions when she felt a sudden strong wind blowing as though a storm were coming up. She looked around and noticed how odd it was that only the branches of the rose bush stirred, nothing else. She made a move toward the river but again was diverted by another gust of wind. No leaf on a tree moved, only those rose branches. She peered hard at the niche, slightly afraid. Her own words best tell the rest of the story:

"Behind those branches, and within the opening, I saw a girl in white, no bigger than myself, who greeted me with a slight bow of her head. At the same time she stretched her arms slightly away from her body, as in pictures of Our Lady. Over her right arm hung a rosary. I was afraid. I stepped back. I wanted to call my friends. I hadn't the courage to do so. I rubbed my eyes again and again. I thought I must be mistaken. . . . She invited me to come nearer. I felt afraid, but not like other fear, for I would have stayed there forever looking at her. . . . I said my rosary. The young girl slipped the beads through her hands, but her lips were not moving.

"While I prayed, I was watching as hard as I could. She was wearing a white dress, a white veil and a blue sash. On each foot I saw a yellow rose. The chain of the rosary was yellow. The beads were white, big and widely spaced. The girl was alive, very young and surrounded with light. When I finished my rosary, she bowed to me and smiled. Then she retired into the niche and disappeared all of a sudden."

This was the first of eighteen appearances over a period of eighteen months. In that year and a half, this previously sheltered young woman, visibly unprepared for the glare of publicity, religious hysteria, lay and clerical skepticism, became the reference point for every kind of reaction from awesome reverence to callous indignity. Bernadette was forced to absorb both the impact of a credulous public as well as the expected and understandable disbelief of the religious and political establishments whose responsibility is the maintenance of public order. Crowds adored her and crowds booed her. Policemen bullied her and clerics intimidated her.

She reacted in most cases as one might expect. Crowds frightened her. Officials made her nervous. With very little schooling and practically no taste for it, Bernadette stumbled and stuttered through the variety of investigations—except when it came to giving a clear, confident and serene account of her religious experiences. When asked to tell what she believed to be the truth, she spoke forthrightly and with unshakable confidence.

Many mystics of the Church had their visions in quiet places—Paul, in the desert; Francis, on a mountain; Gertrude, in a cloister. Bernadette's visions occurred up front for all the world to be aware of. Moreover, the message from the Lady had public consequences: prayer, self-renewal, a church to be built and the siting of a spring that occasioned miracles. But whether in the privacy of a desert solitude or in the publicity of this grotto, all mystics testify that the experience is not programmed; it comes, in the words of Abraham Heschel, as a moment of radical surprise, an event of utter amazement—in Christian language, as a grace. And this is how Bernadette, lacking even the simplest formal knowledge of catechism, analyzed these events. At one level she was upset by the way people treated her, but at another she displayed the rock-hard calm of certitude that her experience was of God.

By the time of her last vision, the tide of tentative acceptance gradually shifted in her favor. The Church sponsored her further education at the convent boarding school of Nevers. This took her at last out of the public eye and gave her some peace. Soon after this she entered the cloister where she spent the rest of her days. Some commentators dwell a bit too dramatically on the resentment and doubt of some of the nuns who could not bring themselves to believe her and thus caused her "untold" suffering. Possibly. But it is more likely that Bernadette judged these events to be minor annoyances. Her inner drive toward Love seems to have given her an accepting and forgiving spirit that put people's reactions in perspective. Her last words reveal something of this: "My Jesus . . . Oh, how I love him. I saw Our Lady. How lovely she was.

How I long to go and see her again." She did so on April 16, 1879. Pius XI canonized her on December 8, 1933, the feast of the Lady who told her she was the "Immaculate Conception."

Reflection

In the words of Eliade, it appears that God "kissed the earth" at Lourdes. Millions have made pilgrimages there and come back better people for it. Bernadette did not have the expected credentials for a mystic or evangelizer of faith, but in the plan of God she worked out very well indeed. At the end of the *Song of Bernadette,* the priest says, "Your life begins, Bernadette." As a saint, the story of her life may prove to be a new beginning for many others as well.

Elizabeth Seton

(1774–1821)

A Responsible
and Loving Woman

"By the law of the church I so much love, I could
never take an obligation which interfered with my
duties to my children."

Elizabeth Seton, Letter to a Friend

The first American Roman Catholic saint was born a
Protestant. Elizabeth Bayley came of old New York
money, WASP traditions and the blessings of the
Episcopal Church. She received an education designed
to fulfill the customary expectations of a woman
destined to take her place as a lady-like person in New
York society. Coming into the world two years before
the writing and publishing of the Declaration of
Independence, this Bayley girl grew up among the
excitements, confusions and shifting alliances that
characterized the years of the American Revolution. As
a doctor for the British army, her father anguished
over divided loyalties, probably being a royalist at
heart, but pragmatically attracted to the new order of
things as the new United States displaced its colonial
status.

At the age of sixteen Elizabeth fell in love with
William Magee Seton, a rich businessman. Three years
later she married William at New York's fashionable
Trinity Church, whose pastor, the formidable Dr. Henry
Hobart found himself strongly attracted to Elizabeth's
evident taste for religion. In quick time Hobart became

a self-appointed spiritual guide for Mrs. Seton and sought to deepen her commitment to Christianity as seen through his "low-Church" or evangelical view of how a good Episcopalian should live. Elizabeth's father was a self-professed humanitarian, showing little interest in organized religion, and had aggressively shared these values with his daughter. (Elizabeth's mother died when she was three.) But Elizabeth was dissatisfied with the limitations of humanitarianism and hungrily sought the fulfillments that religious-based love could provide. Hence she seemed to enjoy the attentions of Dr. Hobart and openly encouraged his efforts to deepen her sense of faith.

Mrs. Seton gave birth to three girls and two boys. In the ninth year of her marriage, a series of woes began to afflict their family. Her husband's business collapsed, and his health along with it. An Italian business acquaintance and longtime friend of the Seton's, the Fillichi family of Leghorn, Italy, invited William, Elizabeth and their oldest daughter to come and live with them, with the idea that this would help William pull himself together and get back on his feet.

Unfortunately, six weeks after their arrival in Italy, William died. The Fillichi's surrounded Elizabeth and young Anna with generous love and care during the mourning period. Their affection as well as their devout Catholicism touched responsive chords in Elizabeth. By the time she was to embark for New York, six months later, Mrs. Seton was well along the way to becoming a convert to the Catholic Church. Antonio Fillichi accompanied the widow and her daughter back to the states, where Elizabeth was joyfully reunited with her other four children, whom she had farmed out with the numerous Bayley-Seton relatives for what was originally to have been a much shorter absence.

Now she was faced with rebuilding her life and pondered her options about how to make a living, or whether to find another husband. The matter was complicated by her growing alienation from the Episcopal Church and her corresponding conviction that she should become a Catholic. Practically speaking this would not be a good move, since it would almost certainly anger her relatives and friends and deprive her of the kind of contacts she would need for survival. That was not an ecumenical age, for the passions that divided Protestants and Catholics in Europe had come across the sea with the respective immigrants. Moreover, the Catholic community was small and without influence, while the Protestant majority constituted the ruling class.

In addition there was the forceful presence of Henry Hobart who now saw it as a matter of honor to conserve Elizabeth's WASP heritage, and who therefore doubled his efforts to tie her loyalties to the Episcopal Church. Elizabeth, however, could not still her conscience, so she pursued her interests in Catholicism and began attending services at St. Peter's Church on Barclay street. Antonio Fillichi, who remained in the states a few months for business reasons, nourished Elizabeth's attraction to Catholicism, providing her with pamphlets and tracts that responded to Protestant objections. Within a year she finally made up her mind and joined the Catholic Church on March 4, 1805, welcomed into it by Father Matthew O'Brien, the pastor of St. Peter's.

Now she was faced with the problem of making a living in earnest, for the traditional doors of support had closed. Early on she had shown an interest in education, partly due to her father's prompting, especially by his sharing with her the teachings of Rousseau. She had not liked Rousseau's a-religious attitudes, but she had agreed with his belief in the values of education and his vision of the inherent riches of each individual, which it was the educator's vocation to draw forth.

Armed with letters of introduction provided by her ever faithful Antonio, Elizabeth proceeded to seek work as a teacher. With one such contact she became a partner in starting a school, but the project soon failed. A second contact proved successful and became the groundwork of a career that would lead her to become the foundress of the American Sisters of Charity and lay the groundwork for the emergence of the Catholic school system in the United States. Father William Du Bourg, superior of the Baltimore Sulpicians, invited her to found a school for girls near St. Mary's Seminary on Paca street.

She accepted the invitation and opened a school that would provide free education for the poor, while taking tuition from those who could afford it. She was soon joined in the effort by the Philadelphia-born Cecelia O'Conway, with whom she began to discuss the possibility of beginning a religious order to stabilize and insure the future of this ministry. Bishop Carroll and Father Du Bourg also had been thinking of this possibility. The concept became a reality within two years.

A property was purchased at Emmitsburg, about fifty miles west of Baltimore. Three other women had shown interest in Elizabeth and Cecelia's dream, and the five of them became the nucleus of the new community, known at first as the Sisters of St. Joseph. As a uniform they chose the garb Mrs. Seton had worn since she became a widow, a black dress with a short cape. They added a white muslin cap, with a fluted border and tied with a black band under the chin. Carroll and Du Bourg recommended they follow an adaptation of the Rule of Vincent de Paul for the Sisters of Charity. They agreed to this and took their vows as the Sisters of Charity of St. Joseph.

Over the next fourteen years, Elizabeth established orphanages in Philadelphia and New York. Compared to some of the other foundresses of religious orders, Elizabeth's accomplishments in terms of numerous foundations were comparatively modest—two schools and two orphanages. She need not have worried, for her successors did all the expanding into colleges, academies, classical high schools, commercial high schools, technical schools, nurse's training schools, general hospitals, TB sanitariums, leper homes, maternity hospitals, nursing homes, infant asylums, day nurseries, Indian schools, retreats for nervous and mental disorders, and so forth. Thousands of her Sisters of Charity work today in North and South America, Italy and many mission countries.

In communicating a vision of social concern, Elizabeth Seton could draw upon two strong influences in her family tradition. Her grandfather, Richard Charlton, had been a curate at Trinity Episcopal in New York, and had dedicated himself to teaching religion to the black slaves of New York City. An early practitioner of a form of integration, he taught his black and white converts side-by-side in the same class. Elizabeth's father, who became the first health officer of New York City, gave more of his time to the poor than to the rich, and lost his life tending the Irish immigrants, having contracted yellow fever from them.

As a young married woman, Elizabeth had created the Widow's Society in New York for the purpose of providing food and clothing for the widows and orphans of the city. She and her sister-in-law, Rebecca, were so identified with such good works that they were often called the "Protestant Sisters of Charity." When her father-in-law died, she took in his six children to raise with her own. Known to be generous and willing, she was frequently called in to help with the sick and the dying.

In other words she was well prepared by background and practice to oversee this new community. She loved working among the sick, the poor, the blacks and disadvantaged groups. She attracted to herself like-minded women and communicated a spirit of selflessness and dedication that would be the hallmark of her "Sisters of Charity." Her outlook may be seen in a letter she wrote to Eliza Sadler:

"You know I am as a mother encompassed by many children of different disposition, not all equally amiable or congenial; but bound to love, instruct and provide for the happiness of all, to give the example of cheerfulness and peace, and consider individuals more as proceeding from the same origin and tending to the same end than in different shades of merit or demerit."

Her busy life included the settling of her family and seeing to their future as well as she could. Antonio helped by arranging an education for the two boys at Georgetown. Her daughters lived with the community and received their education and care until adulthood. Like any mother at that time, Elizabeth worried with a bias about her boys, especially William, whom she tried to make into a banker by sending him to Leghorn to be an apprentice with the Fillichi's. It did not work out. Instead he became a merchant seaman, receiving a steady stream of maternal letters, "Now my love I must hope you are safe in your berth. You must fill a station and take a part in our life of trial, and all your mother can beg is that you keep well with your pilot, and as says Robert Burns, the correspondence fixed with heaven will be your noble anchor." Her son eventually settled down and married and sired sons, one of whom became an Archbishop.

Elizabeth Seton died at the age of forty-five, leaving to the world yet one more important example of a life that can be full of love and that union with Christ is a most desirable state.

The Church canonized her in 1976.

Reflection

It is said that Elizabeth Seton found great spiritual comfort in identifying with the will of God. Her language about God's will can sometimes sound abstract, until one notices the context which is always one of loving concern for others. God's will and God's love were one and the same to her. From her family, her religion and her God she absorbed the supreme lesson of charity. It is the best lesson any saint can teach us.

John Neumann

(1811–1860)

A "Mountain Boy" in Philadelphia

"If you want to be a missionary, you have to love poverty."

John Neumann, A Letter

The Eliot School Controversy was just the kind of affair that motivated John Neumann to fight more vigorously for the building of Catholic schools. He judged rightly that the public schools of his time were, in effect, Protestant schools. They overrode the human and religious rights of Catholic students, forcing them to study the Protestant Bible and participate in Protestant services.

For example, in Boston, 1859, a Catholic family instructed their son at the Eliot School to refuse to read the Protestant Bible or attend school sponsored religious services. The teacher whipped the boy and the parents sued the teacher. The parents lost the case. Moreover, the school district suspended several hundred Catholic students until "all Catholics students learned to obey the rules." Not until the Edgerton, Wisconsin decision of 1890 were Catholic students in public schools excused from such classes and services.

Neumann had sharp words for the public school system: "The school system of the United States is very liberal in theory, but in reality it is most intolerant toward Catholics. Notwithstanding its liberal concessions, it cannot be doubted that the young mind is influenced by the irreligious dispositions of the teacher. Even the textbooks selected for use are injurious to Catholic children. They are nothing less than heretical extracts from a falsified Bible."

Neumann's observations may seem intemperate in our tolerant and ecumenical times, but in the mid-nineteenth century such broadsides between Catholics and Protestants were common enough. To a great extent Neumann was right, for the writers and teachers of the Protestant ruling class did control public school education and the biases that appeared in their textbooks, showing little regard for the sensitivities of Catholics or their rights to a fair view of the facts.

Like many a true, blue immigrant, John Neumann at the age of twenty-five arrived in New York with one suit on his back and one dollar in his pocket. Educated in Budweis, Bohemia, he was a trained seminarian looking for a Bishop to ordain him, for his own country had a surplus of priests. The state of New York needed plenty of priests, so Bishop Dubois was only too happy to ordain this eager young man, sending him off immediately to minister among the German-speaking people in the Buffalo area.

Neumann worked the mission stations with attentive diligence, sometimes running into wild-west style encounters. A fundamentalist minister had drawn him into a public debate about the Bible. Despite his reserved nature and his clumsiness with the English language, Neumann took on the minister and held his own. After the debate a heckler in the audience wanted to continue the dispute. Neumann had no desire to get into a shouting match and began to walk quietly away. His antagonist drew a gun and shouted, "If you don't turn around and talk with me, I'll shoot you." Neumann's response was to keep on walking and ignore the man, leaving the decision in his hands. The heckler put his gun away.

After four years in the Buffalo mission, Neumann decided that he wanted to enter the Redemptorist Order. It was his opinion that he needed the fellowship of a community of priests and the spiritual challenge afforded by a religious order. He was not sure he could endure the isolation of his mission work or bear up under the responsibilities for the long run. "In my faintheartedness, I indulged wild dreams. To escape the terrible responsibilities resting on me, I sometimes thought of abandoning my flock, of fleeing to some distant solitude where I might lead a hidden, penitential life, or hire myself out as a field hand."

He entered the Redemptorist Order in 1840. His novitiate was anything but a time of quiet cloister, for those were pioneer days when there was work to be done and no man to be spared for serving as novice master. In that novitiate year, Neumann served as pastor of St. Philomena's in Pittsburgh, associate pastor of St. Nicholas in New York, a missionary in Buffalo and lastly an administrator in Norwalk, Ohio.

His journal states, "There was no novitiate in America at that time, and no novice master, but an overwhelming amount of work to be done. I daily made two meditations and two examens of conscience, spiritual reading in private, and a visit to the Blessed Sacrament. I recited the rosary also, and that was all." Not quite "all," for the rest of the time he was involved in the various pastoral and missionary works.

Seven years after his entry into the Redemptorists, Neumann was named Superior of the American branch of the Order. It was not the kind of job for which he believed himself suited since he judged he had a poor understanding of financial matters and would rather be the "people's priest" working the parishes than spend hours in administrative tasks. At the same time he was too conscientious a man to avoid responsibilities, so he plunged in as well as he could regarding this new challenge.

It was during this period he developed his interests in Catholic schools. This was augmented by the arrival of the School Sisters of Notre Dame in Baltimore, who sought and obtained from Neumann the moral support they needed to get started. Neumann liked teaching and was apparently very good at it. Mother Caroline reported, "The children often said to me, 'Sister, Father Neumann looked right into my heart.' "

Neumann also knew a little bit about teacher training as Mother Caroline sheepishly confides, "I had a habit of speaking in a high voice and losing my patience while teaching, but after Father Neumann surprised me in this fault once or twice, I learned to correct it. He used to enter the classroom so quietly that I did not notice him until he greeted me with the words, 'Sister, I thought I heard you screaming just now.' " He apparently knew how to correct without offending.

Two years after his appointment as Superior he was relieved of his duties, much to his satisfaction. But within three years he was called to a far more demanding responsibility when the Pope named him the Bishop of Philadelphia. In many ways he was an unlikely choice for this prestigious and complex diocese, the home of the old Quaker establishment and a center for the hordes of Irish immigrants fleeing the potato famine. He would have to preside over a diocese that included half the state of Pennsylvania, all of Delaware and part of New Jersey. He would be the chief pastor for 170,000 Catholics, living in 113 parishes and served by 100 priests. If he had formerly recoiled from administering the needs of forty Redemptorists, he anticipated correctly that life ahead for him had nothing but headaches. It took the strong encouragement of Archbishop Kenrick of Baltimore to persuade him to accept the office.

He possessed few of the ingratiating characteristics that by that time were the normal expectations of

Philadelphians. They wanted to hear a polished and eloquent speaker, but glumly listened to his Bohemian accented English and plain style. The Irish, accustomed only to bishops and pastors from their favorite land, were uncomfortable with this "foreign" bishop. The rich Quaker bankers and businessmen expected to find a quiet and polished gentleman, poised to meet them on their own terms. They found a reticent man, but not one whose breeding was to their taste. The only ones who really liked him from the first were the Germans, because he seemed more like one of them.

Neumann was not indifferent to this cold hospitality from the city of Brotherly Love, but he determined to be himself nonetheless. He led from his strengths, visiting his 117 parishes, opening Catholic schools and paying constant attention to the needs of the poor. Always an exponent of popular devotion, he started the Forty Hours Devotion at St. Phillip Neri Church (whose namesake had begun the practice in Rome) and spread the concept to all the parishes of his diocese. From Philadelphia this devotion expanded to the rest of the country.

Never one to flinch when it was a matter of defending the rights of the Church, Neumann entered heartily into the disputes about "lay trusteeship" in the parishes. Neumann believed that the bishop, representing the Church, should control the ownership of the land and buildings of a parish. Some lay trustees thought otherwise, stating that they should be the owners. Neumann took them to court and lost the first round, but appealed the cases to the state supreme court where he won.

He was less successful on financial matters. This was a "brick and mortar" period of Church development, since buildings were needed for the rapid expansion of Church membership. Big loans were needed and skillful fund raising to meet the debts—as well as a knowledge for financial management. Neumann had enough self insight to realize this was his weakness. Though financial matters had not reached a crisis proportion, they were bad enough to move Neumann to ask for a splitting of the diocese and a personal transfer to a small mission diocese where he could manage things better. Rome partly agreed by reducing the size of the diocese and by giving him an assistant bishop, James Frederick Wood, a convert who had spent years as a banker before becoming a priest. Neumann gratefully put the business administration in Wood's hands and devoted more time to his first love, the pastoral ministry of his people.

At the age of forty-nine, after nine years as Bishop of Philadelphia, the "mountain boy" from Bohemia suffered a fatal heart attack. His wake and funeral drew the normal city-wide attention, large crowds and gatherings of bishops and clergy—with one difference, many of the people sought to clip pieces of his robe as relics. After his burial, people crowded to his tomb to ask for spiritual favors. They were treating him as a saint.

The people persisted through the years. Miracles occurred.

The Church canonized him in 1977.

Reflection

John Neumann was conspicuous for his personal piety and vigorous devotion to pastoral ministry, whether in the mission stations or in the settled areas. Commentators dwell a great deal on his self-effacing lifestyle, but there were qualities about him that drew the top officials of his Order and the Church to choose him to assume the responsibilities of a chief administrator. The record shows him to be a hard working priest. That he was, and more, for he developed an inner life with God, strong enough to solicit popular veneration for his saintliness and official confirmation of this by the Church. It was his faith that made him so. It was the people's faith that realized his saintliness. That is a loving dialogue still available to priests and parishioners alike.

Frances Cabrini

(1850–1917)

An Executive Nun
with A Loving Heart

"Our Lord is my banker. He will not fail to help me find the money."

> *Mother Cabrini, Orphanage Purchase Discussion*

Would a businessman ever cheat a nun? Would a contractor ever take advantage of an Italian immigrant sister trying to build a hospital for the poor? Unexpected perhaps, but this did happen to Frances Cabrini. With the encouragement of Archbishop Quigley she begged enough money to buy the abandoned North Shore Hotel in Chicago for a hospital. The sellers agreed to include lots adjacent to the building, but actually left out that footage in the contract. Frances suspected this and went out and measured the land herself and confronted them with their duplicity, forcing them to back down.

She left the remodeling in charge of some contractors, while she traveled about supervising her missions. A few months later a wire came warning her that she was the victim of fraud. She returned to a mess of a building and a $40,000 debt, discovering that her trusted contractors were tearing things apart and charging her three times too much for the work. She roared at them and commented, "This moment I could devour them alive."

She checked out the blueprints with some consulting engineers and evaluated the damage. Wasting no time she brought the contractors to her lawyers and accused them of damages and fraud, fired them and said she would see them later in court. "I will serve as building supervisor and finish the job." She was as good as her word, going to the Italian district and recruiting bricklayers, carpenters, plumbers, and so forth. From dawn to dusk she was there until her dream building came true, Columbus Hospital.

This spirited woman was born in Italy, the youngest of thirteen children. As a child she felt the call to be a nun and applied several times to religious orders, but was refused. At the age of twenty-four, she offered her services to the Providence House Orphanage in Codogno, at the bidding of her spiritual adviser. The house was financed and run by an eccentric Antonia Tondini and a friend, Teresa Calza. Frances found chaos at Providence, dirt, poorly cooked meals, no education or spiritual training for the orphans. Worse yet, the two women in charge passed their evenings getting drunk and quarreling and arbitrarily beating the orphans when it suited them.

It was the bishop's idea that, with the arrival of Frances, he would make the three women nuns. Perhaps that would put some sense of responsibility into Tondini and Calza, with Frances serving as the upbeat influence. The bishop was one-third right. Over the next three years Frances organized the orphan girls, taught them, washed the house, helped them to pray, all the while putting up with the relentless opposition of the other two. Frances refused to become a nun with them, telling the bishop that her ultimate intention was to become a missionary.

After three years of this, Frances found that seven of the girls would be willing to join her as nuns in a proposed missionary order. The bishop agreed and created the Missionary Sisters of the Sacred Heart. For yet three more years, incredibly, Frances and her sisters lived in that Providence madhouse, until the bishop was convinced that the diocese should buy new property and move the orphanage and the new order there.

Frances proceeded to open six other orphanages and watched her order grow. She obtained an audience with Leo XIII to get his backing for a foundation in China. The Pope said, "No, the house and family of western civilization must be put in order first. His love must conquer the West before we approach the East. America will soon achieve world influence. If she becomes another soulless Babylon, she will topple, and with her fall she will drag down lesser nations, and the Christian labors of centuries. Frances Cabrini, go to America."

Frances was aware that thousands of Italians were migrating to the United States, Brazil and Argentina and concurred with the Pope that the Church must follow them, if their faith was to be kept alive. She sailed to New York with six of her sisters, assured that a new orphanage awaited their services there. She was wrong, for the deal had fallen through and news of it arrived too late in Italy. Archbishop Corrigan tried to explain the complexities of American life and suggested they open a school for Italian children at San Gioacchino's Church. Frances and the six sisters could be housed by the Irish Sisters of Charity.

Wasting no time, Frances marched her sisters to the church and set up "classrooms" all over the building. She had no trouble getting students whose families enthusiastically brought their young for training in basic skills and religion. Barely settled in, Frances found out she could be an aggressive and successful beggar for funds to open the orphanage. She went to the Countess Cesnola, who had raised the orphanage idea originally, and persuaded her that the concept would work. The Countess would provide a house and God would provide the rest. The two of them convinced the archbishop and Frances got her orphanage.

Frances and her sisters went everywhere seeking help from butchers, bakers, vegetable and fruit stand owners, clothing store merchants, the homes of the poor and the mansions of the rich. They wheedled, pleaded, cajoled and coaxed out of people the money and clothing and food they needed to keep the orphanage going. Frances, or Mother Cabrini as everyone called her, began to see that the house on 59th Street was not the best place for children. They needed fresh air and a place to run around. She looked enviably at the 450 acre Jesuit property across the river, and when she found out it was for sale she put in the first bid. The Jesuits told her they were moving because there was no water there, other than what could be brought up from the river. Nothing deterred her. She found money to buy the property and moved her orphans to the country. They washed clothes in the river and set up bucket brigades to bring water to the house. And wouldn't you know it, Mother Cabrini found a well on the property. This thirty-year-old immigrant nun accomplished all this within one year of her arrival in New York.

Back to Rome from one of the thirty Atlantic crossings that would mark her lifetime, she received an invitation to open a house in Nicaragua. The idea intrigued her and she sailed for that Central American country and established a school there. On her way back to New York she stopped off in New Orleans where she shared the grief of the Italian community mourning yet the lynching of eleven Italian men. With the aid of the Archbishop she made arrangements for opening an Italian parish, for which she would provide a school and an orphanage.

Upon her return to New York it became clear to her that the city needed a hospital for poor Italians, and poor people in general. The well-intentioned Scalabrini Fathers had opened one, but it was poorly managed and on the brink of closing. She thought of joining with them, but things did not work out. She rented two homes and started a ten bed makeshift hospital, carrying in water, bringing soup from a restaurant, begging blankets and sheets, some twenty bottles of antiseptics and some packages of gauze, cotton and adhesives—meanwhile keeping creditors at bay.

She knew she needed big money to get a real start, so she presented her case urgently and convincingly to businessmen (not the kind she met in Chicago), who saw in her the talents of an executive and were willing to grant her long-term credit. A retired pasta manufacturer volunteered his services as a business manager, sometimes paying the debts with his own money. She called him, "my sweet old uncle who does not fail his Lord." A prominent doctor, named Keane, volunteered to be head of staff, donating his time, talents, money and instruments. Other doctors, Protestant and Jewish as well as Catholics, donated their services as well. There were free wards for the poor and space for the rich who helped pay for the poor. The Italian poor could count on home-cooked Italian meals and their much beloved wines.

Mother Cabrini had launched the first of her "Columbus Hospitals" a pattern that was to be repeated in Chicago, Denver, Los Angeles, Philadelphia, Seattle and New Orleans. For a supposedly frail woman, she had a rugged capacity for travel in a time when traveling was a challenge to the hardiest of souls. She disliked sea travel because she had a fear of drowning, but off she went over the oceans dozens of times, checking out her houses in Italy, France and England, then sailing to Brazil and Argentina where she again found Italian communities in need of her unique services and cheerful presence.

Trains and boats of the period were enough to wear anyone down, but what about a mule trip across the

Andes? A mule trip? Yes, how else is one to get from Santiago, Chile to Buenos Aires, Argentina? She could have taken the boat around Cape Horn, but instead decided to ride by mule across the mountains just as the snows were melting. She nearly died, not from the rigors of the trip but by slipping in a jump across a crevice, but saved just in time by a watchful muleteer.

Mother Cabrini's ministerial years are a fast forward blur of perpetual motion, now deep in the Denver mines to visit and comfort the Italian miners, now standing at the scaffold and holding onto the hands of Italian prisoners about to be hanged, praying with them and encouraging them, now on a boat or train or mule. She came to New York when she was thirty and died in Chicago thirty-seven years later. No aspect of life was too unimportant for her from washing dishes to paying bills to spending hours scouting a city to find just the right place for another hospital or orphanage. She rode in fancy carriages and plain street cars, the vehicle making no difference to her, as her active and fertile mind kept on planning for the maintenance and development of her projects.

She sat in the executive suites of the captains of industry, the quiet parlors of archbishops and the plain homes of the Little Italies of America. All for one purpose, that the love of Christ be made manifest to those in need. She brought her people ethnic pride before the intellectuals had coined the phrase. She left behind sixty-seven houses and 1,500 Missionary Sisters of the Sacred Heart.

Having become a United States citizen in 1909, she was the first such person to be canonized a saint by Pius XII in 1946.

Reflection

The adjectives come easily when thinking about Mother Cabrini—bold, risk-taking, committed, loving, tireless, and so forth. She represented many of the values that we look for in humanitarians, and more so, in saints. Her single-mindedness was awesome, her executive abilities the envy of any manager and her prayerful love just the tonic we wish for in religious leaders today. Italian Americans could not be happier than to have a woman like this reflect their ethnic greatness. The rest of us are pretty proud too.